# 504

# ABSOLUTELY ESSENTIAL

# WORDS

## THIRD EDITION

Murray Bromberg, Director, New York City SUPERCENTER

Julius Liebb, Former Assistant Principal, Andrew Jackson H.S.

Arthur Traiger, Former Assistant Principal, Martin Van Buren H.S.

Instructor, Japan University

**BARRON'S**

EDUCATIONAL SERIES, INC.

New York • London • Toronto • Sydney

# Table of Contents

### Pronunciation Guide

The pronunciation of the *504 absolutely essential words* included in this book are those used by educated, cultured speakers in everyday, relaxed, informal conversation.

Below are a list of symbols; the sound that each symbol represents can be easily understood from the key word in which it is shown.

| | | | | | | | |
|---|---|---|---|---|---|---|---|
| a | back | ô | horn | f | fall | s | sit |
| ā | hay | oo | look | g | get | t | tin |
| ä | car | o͞o | too | h | hotel | v | voice |
| ã | care | oi | toy | j | joy | w | win |
| e | then | u | up | k | kill | ch | church |
| ē | easy | ù | toot | l | let | hw | white |
| ė | bird | ū | you | m | man | zh | leisure |
| i | it | ou | out | n | not | y | yes |
| ī | kite | b | bed | p | put | z | zebra |
| ō | home | d | done | r | rose | ŋ | drink |

The unstressed vowel sound is symbolized as follows:

ə    for **a** as in around        for **o** as in complete
      for **e** as in glitter           for **u** as in focus
      for **i** as in sanity

ANSWERS TO ALL EXERCISES ARE ON PAGES 134 - 136

# Introduction

This is a self-help book. If you use it intelligently, you will help yourself to strengthen and expand your word knowledge. The words you will learn, moreover, are essential in that they are known and used regularly by educated people. You will find that such words as *squander, rehabilitate, blunder, obesity* and five hundred more will turn up in your newspapers, in the magazines you read, in books, on television, in the movies, and in the conversation of the people you meet daily.

**504 Absolutely Essential Words** is divided into forty-two lessons, each containing twelve new words. Those words are first presented to you in three sample sentences; next, the new words appear in a brief article; the last part of each lesson is a set of exercises that give you practice using the new words. One of the most important features of **504...Words** is that each of the new words is repeated over and over again throughout this book so that you will have a greater chance to become familiar with it.

Newly added are seven Word Review sections, each containing challenging exercises that will help you to test your mastery of the new words.

# How To Use This Book

**504 Absolutely Essential Words** can be used in a number of ways, depending upon the needs and the status of the reader. A student in a high school English class, for example, could work with the book over a period of one school year, learning a dozen words each week for forty-two weeks. Pupils who are studying vocabulary in an individualized program can move through the text at their own speed, mastering the new words as rapidly as they are able. Adults, out of school, can dip into the book on a selective basis, paying attention to the new words and skipping over those with which they are already familiar.

*The High School English Class*   Some teachers prefer to set aside one day a week for intensive vocabulary study. At such time the sentences containing the new words are often read aloud so that the pupils hear them used in context. The definitions may be copied into a vocabulary notebook to reinforce the learning. Next, the accompanying paragraph(s) containing the twelve new words should be read aloud, followed by the exercise in which the blanks are to be filled in. Some discussion of the "Spotlight on" word is appropriate, preceding a homework assignment in which the students compose original sentences for each of the new words.

*Independent Study*   An interesting way to approach **504 Absolutely Essential Words** on one's own is to take an informal pre-test on each week's words, comparing the definitions with the ones provided in the text. After studying the three sample sentences, the reader should compose several original ones, using the model paragraph(s) for resource material.

The "Spotlight on" word introduces students to the fascinating history of the English language. They are advised to look up other words in each lesson in order to find out about their origin and to expand their vocabulary in the process.

Finally, students who are working on their own should complete the exercises at the end of each section, filling in the blanks and striving for a perfect score.

*Repetition*   The words with asterisks (*) are those which have been taught in previous lessons. They are planted everywhere in the book since the repetition of newly-learned material is a recognized road to mastery. If you come across such a word but cannot remember its meaning, turn back to the lesson in which that word first appeared. (See the index on pages 137 and 138 for such information.)

# Lesson 1

*"All words are pegs to hang ideas on."*

Henry Ward Beecher, *Proverbs from Plymouth Pulpit*

1. **abandon** (ə ban′ dən) desert; leave without planning to come back; quit
   a. When Roy **abandoned** his family, the police went looking for him.
   b. The soldier could not **abandon** his friends who were hurt in battle.
   c. Because Rose was poor, she had to **abandon** her idea of going to college.

2. **keen** (kēn) sharp; eager; intense; sensitive
   a. The butcher's **keen** knife cut through the meat.
   b. My dog has a **keen** sense of smell.
   c. Bill's **keen** mind pleased all his teachers.

3. **jealous** (jel′ əs) afraid that the one you love might prefer someone else; wanting what someone else has
   a. A detective was hired by the **jealous** widow to find the boyfriend who had abandoned* her.
   b. Although my neighbor just bought a new car, I am not **jealous** of him.
   c. Being **jealous,** Mona would not let her boyfriend dance with any of the cheerleaders.

4. **tact** (takt) ability to say the right thing
   a. My aunt never hurts anyone's feelings because she always uses **tact.**
   b. By the use of **tact,** Janet was able to calm her jealous* husband.
   c. Your friends will admire you if you use **tact** and thoughtfulness.

5. **oath** (ōth) a promise that something is true; a curse
   a. The President will take the **oath** of office tomorrow.
   b. In court, the witness took an **oath** that he would tell the whole truth.
   c. When Terry discovered that he had been abandoned,* he let out an angry **oath.**

6. **vacant** (vā′ kənt) empty; not filled
   a. Someone is planning to build a house on that **vacant** lot.
   b. I put my coat on that **vacant** seat.
   c. When the landlord broke in, he found that apartment **vacant.**

7. **hardship** (härd′ ship) something that is hard to bear; difficulty
   a. The fighter had to face many **hardships** before he became champion.
   b. Abe Lincoln was able to overcome one **hardship** after another.
   c. On account of **hardship,** Bert was let out of the army to take care of his sick mother.

8. **gallant** (gal′ ənt) brave; showing respect for women
   a. The pilot swore a **gallant** oath* to save his buddy.
   b. Many **gallant** knights entered the contest to win the princess.
   c. Ed is so **gallant** that he always gives up his subway seat to a woman.

9. **data** (dāt′ ə or dat′ ə) facts; information
   a. The **data** about the bank robbery were given to the F.B.I.
   b. After studying the **data,** we were able to finish our report.
   c. Unless you are given all the **data** , you cannot do the math problem.

10. **unaccustomed** (ən ə kəs ′ təmd) not used to something
    a. Coming from Alaska, Claude was **unaccustomed** to Florida's heat.
    b. The king was **unaccustomed** to having people disobey him.
    c. **Unaccustomed** as he was to exercise, Vic quickly became tired.

11. **bachelor** (batch′ ə lər) a man who has not married
    a. My brother took an oath* to remain a **bachelor.**
    b. In the movie, the married man was mistaken for a **bachelor.**
    c. Before the wedding, all his **bachelor** friends had a party.

12. **qualify** (kwäl ə-ˌfī) become fit; show that you are able
    a.  I am trying to **qualify** for the job which is now vacant.*
    b.  Since Pauline can't carry a tune, she is sure that she will never **qualify** for the Girls Chorus.
    c.  You have to be over 5′5″ to **qualify** as a policeman.

*Read the following story to see how the new words are used in it.*

### My Brother, the Gentleman

The story of Sir Walter Raleigh who spread his cloak on the ground to keep Queen Elizabeth from the **hardship** of crossing a muddy puddle can **qualify** that nobleman for an award as a man of **tact** and good breeding. My brother Kenny, a **bachelor** with a **keen** interest in history, was impressed by that anecdote and thought he might demonstrate his excellent upbringing in a parallel situation. Accordingly he decided to **abandon** his subway seat in favor of a woman standing nearby.

Although **unaccustomed** to such generous treatment, the young woman was pleased to accept Kenny's kind offer. However, her **jealous** boyfriend swore an **oath** under his breath because he thought my brother was flirting with his girlfriend. I don't have any **data** on the number of young men who get into similar trouble as a result of a **gallant** gesture, but it's probably one in a thousand. Poor Kenny! He pointed to the now **vacant** seat.

**Which of the words studied in this lesson is suggested by the picture?**

**Place one of the new words in each of the blanks below.**

1.  As I looked at all the _____ which the salesman showed me, I knew that I was getting more and more mixed up.
2.  I used _____ when I told my fat uncle that his extra weight made him look better.
3.  When the guard saw that the cot was _____, he realized that the prisoner had left the jail.
4.  Although he took an _____ on the Bible, Sal lied to the jury.
5.  My aunt was so _____ of our new couch that she bought one just like it.
6.  I enjoyed reading the story of the _____ man who put his cloak over a mud puddle so that the queen would not dirty her feet.
7.  The loss of Claudia's eyesight was a _____ which she learned to live with.
8.  The driver was forced to _____ his car when two of the tires became flat.
9.  Betty could not _____ for the Miss Teenage America Contest because she was twenty years old.
10. The blade was so _____ that I cut myself in four places while shaving.
11. _____ to being kept waiting, the angry woman marched out of the store.
12. Because he was a _____, the movie actor was invited to many parties.

---

**Which Word Means.** From the list of 12 new words that follows, choose the one that corresponds to each definition below.

| | | | |
|---|---|---|---|
| abandon | keen | jealous | tact |
| oath | vacant | hardship | gallant |
| data | unaccustomed | bachelor | qualify |

1. a promise that something is true _____
2. sharp; eager; intense _____
3. to desert; to leave without planning to come back _____
4. something that is hard to bear _____
5. to become fit _____
6. wanting what someone else has _____
7. brave; showing respect for women _____
8. a man who has not married _____
9. facts; information _____
10. the ability to say the right thing _____
11. empty; not filled _____
12. not used to something _____

---

**Spotlight on:**  **abandon** — This is an interesting word with a French background; in that language it meant "to put under another's control," hence, "to give up." In Lesson 19 you will find the new word *ban*, and may discover how it is related to *abandon*. A good dictionary will also show you the connection with other words such as *bandit* and *contraband*.

# Lesson 2

"Alice had not the slightest idea what Latitude was, or Longitude either, but she thought they were nice grand words to say."

Lewis Carroll, *Alice's Adventures in Wonderland*

1. **corpse** (kôrps) a dead body, usually of a person
   a. When given all the data* on the **corpse,** Charlie Chan was able to solve the murder.
   b. The **corpse** was laid to rest in the vacant* coffin.
   c. An oath* of revenge was sworn over the **corpse** by his relatives.

2. **conceal** (kən sēl') hide
   a. Tris could not **conceal** his love for Gloria.
   b. Count Dracula **concealed** the corpse* in his castle.
   c. The money was so cleverly **concealed** that we were forced to abandon* our search for it.

3. **dismal** (diz' məl) dark and depressing
   a. When the weather is so **dismal,** I sometimes stay in bed all day.
   b. I am unaccustomed* to this **dismal** climate.
   c. As the **dismal** reports of the election came in, the senator's friends tactfully* made no mention of them.

4. **frigid** (frij' id) very cold
   a. It was a great hardship* for the men to live through the **frigid** winter at Valley Forge.
   b. The jealous* bachelor* was treated in a **frigid** manner by his girlfriend.
   c. Inside the butcher's freezer the temperature was **frigid.**

5. **inhabit** (in hab' it) live in
   a. Eskimos **inhabit** the frigid* part of Alaska.
   b. Because Sidney qualified,* he was allowed to **inhabit** the vacant* apartment.
   c. Many crimes are committed each year against those who **inhabit** the slum area of our city.

6. **numb** (num) without the power of feeling; deadened
   a. My fingers quickly became **numb** in the frigid* room.
   b. A **numb** feeling came over Mr. Massey as he read the telegram.
   c. When the nurse stuck a pin in my **numb** leg, I felt nothing.

7. **peril** (per' əl) danger
   a. The hunter was abandoned* by the natives when he described the **peril** which lay ahead of them.
   b. There is great **peril** in trying to climb the mountain.
   c. Our library is filled with stories of **perilous** adventures.

8. **recline** (ri klīn') lie down; stretch out; lean back
   a. Richard likes to **recline** in front of the television set.
   b. After **reclining** on her right arm for an hour, Maxine found that it had become numb.*
   c. My dog's greatest pleasure is to **recline** by the warm fireplace.

9. **shriek** (shrēk) scream
   a. The maid **shrieked** when she discovered the corpse.*
   b. With a loud **shriek,** Ronald fled from the room.
   c. Facing the peril* of the waterfall, the boatman let out a terrible **shriek.**

10. **sinister** (sin' is tər) evil; wicked; dishonest; frightening
    a. The **sinister** plot to cheat the widow was uncovered by the police.
    b. When the bank guard spied the **sinister**-looking customer, he drew his gun.
    c. I was frightened by the **sinister** shadow at the bottom of the stairs.

11. **tempt** (tempt) try to get someone to do something; test; invite
    a. A banana split can **tempt** me to break my diet.
    b. The sight of beautiful Louise **tempted** the bachelor* to change his mind about marriage.
    c. Your offer of a job **tempts** me greatly.
12. **wager** (wā′ jər) bet
    a. I lost a small **wager** on the Superbowl.
    b. After winning the **wager**, Tex treated everyone to free drinks.
    c. It is legal to make a **wager** in the state of Nevada.

*Read the following story to see how the new words are used in it.*

### Terror In the Cemetery

I like to bet on anything that is exciting, so when my friends tried to **tempt** me with an offer, I took it. The idea was for me to spend a **frigid** December night in a cemetery, all alone, in order to win twenty dollars. Little did I realize that they would use dirty tricks to try to frighten me to abandon* the cemetery and, therefore, lose my **wager**.

My plan was to **recline** in front of a large grave, covered by a warm blanket, with a flashlight to help me cut through the **dismal** darkness. After midnight, I heard a wild **shriek**. I thought I saw the grave open and a **corpse** rise out of it! Although I was somewhat **numb** with fear, I tried to keep my senses. Using good judgment, I knew that no **peril** could come to me from that **sinister** figure. When I did not run in terror, my friends, who had decided to **conceal** themselves behind the nearby tombstones, came out and we all had a good laugh. Those spirits which may **inhabit** a cemetery must have had a good laugh, too.

### Place one of the new words in each of the blanks below.

1. The chances of my winning the election were so _____ that I decided to quit before the votes were counted.
2. I won the _____ that my bachelor* friend would be married by June.
3. Kit Carson's keen* eyesight protected him from the _____ in the forest.
4. While escaping from the bank, the robbers forced the teller to _____ on the floor of their car.
5. Since the shack was vacant,* we did not expect to hear the terrible _____ which came from it.
6. With a _____ smile, the gangster invited Martha into his Cadillac.
7. You cannot _____ the truth when you are questioned by the keen* lawyer.
8. It is said that many ghosts _____ the old Butler house.
9. In _____ weather I always wear three or four sweaters.
10. After standing guard duty for four hours, I became completely _____.
11. As the closet was opened, the _____ fell out, frightening the janitor out of one year's growth.
12. With the promise of a rise in pay, my boss tried to _____ me to stay on in the job.

### Exercise
*Now make up your own sentences, one for each of the new words you have just been taught.*

1. _____
2. _____
3. _____
4. _____
5. _____
6. _____

7. _____

8. _____

9. _____

10. _____

11. _____

12. _____

_____

**Spotlight on:**   **sinister**—in Latin this word means "on the left." According to ancient belief, that which appeared on the left-hand side brought bad luck. Another explanation for connecting bad luck with the left side is that the west (left) is toward the setting sun.

**Which of the words studied in this lesson is suggested by the picture?**

# Lesson 3

"Good words anoint a man, ill words kill a man."

John Florio, *First Fruites*

## Words To Learn This Week

typical
minimum
scarce
annual
persuade
essential
blend
visible
expensive
beau
devise
wholesale

1. **typical** (tip′ ə kəl) usual; of a kind
   a. The sinister* character in the movie wore a **typical** costume, a dark shirt, loud tie, and tight jacket.
   b. The horse ran its **typical** race, a slow start and a slower finish, and I lost my wager.*
   c. It was **typical** of the latecomer to conceal* the real cause of his lateness.

2. **minimum** (min′ ə məm) the least possible amount; the lowest amount
   a. Studies show that adults need a **minimum** of six hours sleep.
   b. The **minimum** charge for a telephone, even if no calls are made, is about nine dollars a month.
   c. Congress has set a **minimum** wage for all workers.

3. **scarce** (skãrs) hard to get; rare
   a. Chairs which are older than one hundred years are **scarce.**
   b. Because there is little moisture in the desert, trees are **scarce.**
   c. How **scarce** are good cooks?

4. **annual** (an′ ūəl) once a year; something that appears yearly or lasts for a year
   a. The **annual** convention of musicians takes place in Hollywood.
   b. The publishers of the encyclopedia put out a book each year called an **annual.**
   c. Plants that live only one year are called **annuals.**

5. **persuade** (pər swād′) win over to do or believe; make willing
   a. Can you **persuade** him to give up his bachelor* days and get married?
   b. No one could **persuade** the captain to leave the sinking ship.
   c. Beth's shriek* **persuaded** Jesse that she was in real danger.

6. **essential** (ə sen′ shəl) necessary; very important
   a. The **essential** items in the cake are flour, sugar, and shortening.
   b. It is **essential** that we follow the road map.
   c. Several layers of thin clothing are **essential** to keeping warm in frigid* climates.

7. **blend** (blend) mix together thoroughly; a mixture
   a. The colors of the rainbow **blend** into one another.
   b. A careful **blend** of fine products will result in delicious food.
   c. When Jose **blends** the potatoes together, they come out very smooth.

8. **visible** (viz′ ə bəl) able to be seen
   a. The ship was barely **visible** through the dense fog.
   b. Before the stars are **visible,** the sky has to become quite dark.
   c. You need a powerful lens to make some germs **visible.**

9. **expensive** (eks pen′ səv) costly; high-priced
   a. Because diamonds are scarce* they are **expensive.**
   b. Margarine is much less **expensive** than butter.
   c. Shirley's **expensive** dress created a great deal of excitement at the party.

10. **beau** (bō) boyfriend; suitor
    a. When her **beau** talked to other girls, Diane became jealous.*
    b. Even if you have no **beau,** you are welcome at the dance.
    c. Miss Evans and her **beau** went shopping for furniture.

11. **devise** (də vīz′) think out; plan; invent
    a. The burglars **devised** a scheme for entering the bank at night.
    b. I would like to **devise** a method for keeping my toes from becoming numb* while I am ice skating.
    c. If we could **devise** a plan for using the abandoned* building, we could save thousands of dollars.
12. **wholesale** (hōl′ sāl) in large quantity; less than retail in price
    a. The **wholesale** price of milk is six cents a quart lower than retail.
    b. Many people were angered by the **wholesale** slaughter of birds.
    c. By buying my ties **wholesale** I save fifteen dollars a year.

---

*Read the following story to see how the new words are used in it.*

## Start Saving for Sable

You have just won first prize in a lottery, and you need a new winter coat. How about a sable fur coat? A sable coat may be **expensive**, but it is soft, light, and warm.

A **typical** sable coat costs more than a Cadillac, as much as an education at a good college, more even than some inexpensive homes. Why? A **minimum** of sixty **scarce** little pelts, at nearly $600 per pelt, go into each coat. Fur merchants gather each year in frigid* Leningrad, Russia, to bid for the furs at the **annual** auction there. Then the furs are shipped to America and processed in chemicals and oils until soft. After the customer chooses the skins for her coat, the dismal* pro-

cess of matching begins — a long but **essential** job. Each coat is made from a bundle of skins that ranges from light to dark in color, and the skins have to **blend** so that the seams are not **visible**. Finally, the coat is styled and finished.

If you don't win a lottery, see if you can **persuade** your **beau** to **devise** a way to get a sable coat for you **wholesale.** Oh, well, you can always wear an extra sweater or two if it gets really cold this winter, and knowing that sixty innocent animals did not die in order to make you a coat may help to keep you warm.

---

## Place one of the new words in each of the blanks below.

1. The March of Dimes makes its _____ appeal in the early spring.
2. Oil paints _____ easily to form thousands of different shades.
3. The _____ passing mark in most schools is 65%.
4. Since we have been invited by couples, I'll ask my _____ to accompany me.
5. Your gifts do not tempt* me and will not _____ me to change my mind.
6. In the cemetery the corpse* was _____ in the bright moonlight.
7. A _____ day in Florida is full of sunshine and warm breezes.
8. Let's _____ a plan for doing away with homework.
9. Everyone agrees that friendship is _____ for all of us.
10. A sharp rise in _____ prices is bound to affect the prices in our neighborhood stores.
11. The buffalo which once roamed the plains is quite _____ today.
12. Government experts told us to buy chicken without realizing how _____ it had become.

---

## Exercise

*Now make up your own sentences, one for each of the new words you have just been taught.*

1. _____

2. _____

3. _____

4. _____

5. _____

6. _____

7. _____

8. _____

9. _____

10. _____

11. _____

12. _____

**Spotlight on:**    **expensive**—The definition given to you was "costly, high-priced." Other synonyms could have been provided because English is quite rich in that area. Webster's *Dictionary of Synonyms*, for example, contains ten entries which explain *expensive* or show us slight variations of the word: *costly, dear, valuable, precious, invaluable, priceless, exorbitant, excessive, immoderate*. When would you use *costly* as a synonym for *expensive* and when would you use *excessive*?

**Which of the words studied in this lesson is suggested by the picture?**

# Lesson 4

"Good words are worth much and cost little."

George Herbert, *Jacula Prudentum*

**Words To Learn This Week**

vapor
eliminate
villain
dense
utilize
humid
theory
descend
circulate
enormous
predict
vanish

1. **vapor** (vā′ pər) moisture in the air that can be seen; fog; mist
   a. Scientists have devised* methods for trapping **vapor** in bottles so they can study its make-up.
   b. He has gathered data* on the amount of **vapor** rising from the swamp.
   c. A **vapor** trail is the visible* stream of moisture left by the engines of a jet flying at high altitudes.

2. **eliminate** (i lim′ ə nāt) get rid of; remove; omit
   a. When the railroad tracks are raised, the danger of crossing will be **eliminated.**
   b. When figuring the cost of a car, **eliminate** such extras as air conditioning.
   c. If we were to **eliminate** all reclining* chairs, no one would fall asleep while watching television.

3. **villain** (vil′ ən) a very wicked person
   a. A typical* moving picture **villain** gets killed at the end.
   b. The **villain** concealed* the corpse* in the cellar.
   c. When the **villain** fell down the well, everyone lived happily ever after.

4. **dense** (dens) closely packed together; thick
   a. The **dense** leaves on the trees let in a minimum* of sunlight.
   b. We couldn't row because of the **dense** weeds in the lake.
   c. His keen* knife cut through the **dense** jungle.

5. **utilize** (ū′ tə līz) make use of
   a. No one seems willing to **utilize** this vacant* house.
   b. The gardener was eager to **utilize** different flowers and blend* them in order to beautify the borders.
   c. Does your mother **utilize** leftovers in her cooking?

6. **humid** (hū′ mid) moist; damp
   a. It was so **humid** in our classroom that we wished the school would buy an air conditioner.
   b. New Yorkers usually complain in the summer of the **humid** air.
   c. Most people believe that ocean air is quite **humid.**

7. **theory** (thē′ ə rē) explanation based on thought, observation, or reasoning
   a. Einstein's **theory** is really too difficult for the average person to understand.
   b. My uncle has a **theory** about the effect of weather on baseball batters.
   c. No one has advanced a **theory** explaining the beginnings of writing.

8. **descend** (di send′) go or come down from a higher place to a lower level
   a. If we let the air out of a balloon, it will have to **descend.**
   b. The pilot, thinking his plane was in peril,* **descended** quickly.
   c. Knowing her beau* was waiting at the bottom of the staircase, Eleanor **descended** at once.

9. **circulate** (sər′ kū lāt) go around; go from place to place or person to person
   a. A fan may **circulate** the air in summer, but it doesn't cool it.
   b. My father **circulated** among the guests at the party and made them feel comfortable.
   c. Hot water **circulates** through the pipes in the building, keeping the room warm.

10. **enormous** (i nôr′ məs) extremely large; huge
    a. The **enormous** crab moved across the ocean floor in search of food.
    b. Public hangings once drew **enormous** crowds.
    c. The gallant* knight drew his sword and killed the **enormous** dragon.

11. **predict** (pri dikt') tell beforehand
   a.  Weathermen can **predict** the weather correctly most of the time.
   b.  Who can **predict** the winner of the Superbowl this year?
   c.  Laura thought she could **predict** what I would do, but she was wrong.
12. **vanish** (van' ish) disappear; disappear suddenly
   a.  Even in California the sun will sometimes **vanish** behind a cloud.
   b.  Not even a powerful witch can make a jealous* lover **vanish.**
   c.  Give him a week without a job and all his money will **vanish.**

*Read the following story to see how the new words are used in it.*

### A Fan in the Air

Fog, tiny droplets of water **vapor,** is the **villain** of the airports. In an effort to **eliminate dense** fog from airports, weathermen **utilize** giant fans, nylon strings, and chemicals dropped from planes or shot upwards from strange machines on the ground. Nothing works as well, though, as a new weapon in the fight against fog: the helicopter. Researchers believe that if warm dry air above the fog could somehow be driven down into the **humid** blanket of fog, the droplets would evaporate, thus clearing the air. In a recent experiment to test their **theory** the researchers had a helicopter **descend** into the fog above barely visible* Smith Mountain Airport near Roanoke, Virginia. The blades of the helicopter caused the air to **circulate** downwards and an **enormous** hole in the clouds opened above the airport. Weathermen **predict** that with larger, more expensive* helicopters they will be able to make the thickest fog **vanish.**

**Which of the words studied in this lesson is suggested by the picture?**

**Place one of the new words in each of the blanks below.**

1. If we have one more hot, _____ day, you will be able to persuade* me to move to Alaska.
2. In the show the magician waved his wand to make a lady _____ .
3. The hair on his head was so _____, a special pair of scissors was used to thin it.
4. Since he has passed all his subjects, I'll _____ that he will graduate.
5. The _____ in the movie was played by an actor who was able to look mean.
6. _____ rose out of the valve on top of the steam engine.
7. The basketball player was _____; he could practically drop the ball through the hoop.
8. What _____ can you suggest to explain the frequent changes in women's clothing?
9. Why don't you _____ all the space on that page?
10. Sooner or later the elevator will _____ and we'll be able to go up.
11. I heard a doctor on a television show say that if we _____ one slice of bread each day, we'll lose weight.
12. Copies of some magazines are so scarce,* the librarian won't allow them to _____ .

---

**Synonyms.** Circle the word that most nearly expresses the meaning of the word printed in heavy black type.

1. **circulate** the news
   (a) report    (b) spread    (c) interpret    (d) watch
2. **eliminate** a problem
   (a) perceive    (b) wipe out    (c) aggravate    (d) create
3. an **enormous** ocean liner
   (a) incredible    (b) extravagant    (c) unforgettable    (d) huge
4. **dense** fog
   (a) misty    (b) thick    (c) invisible    (d) dismal*
5. **descend** the stairs
   (a) slip on    (b) fortify    (c) come down    (d) use
6. the suspected **villain**
   (a) wicked person    (b) schemer    (c) gossip    (d) dictator
7. **humid** climate
   (a) frigid*    (b) moist    (c) perilous*    (d) sunny
8. **predict** the future
   (a) plan for    (b) look forward to    (c) foretell    (d) accept
9. deadly **vapors** from the chemical explosion
   (a) forces    (b) explosives    (c) gases    (d) sleet
10. **vanish** into thin air
    (a) change    (b) crumble    (c) disappear    (d) vacate
11. science **theory**
    (a) knowledge of facts    (b) laboratory equipment
    (c) explanation based on thought    (d) experiment
12. **utilize** their services
    (a) pay for    (b) make use of    (c) extend    (d) regain

**Spotlight on:**    **villain**—We see from this how social attitudes can affect the meanings of words. In Latin a *villa* was a small farm and its buildings; a connection of such buildings became a *village*, and a person who lived on such a farm was a *villain*. Some who lived in the cities looked down on the country folk, regarding them as stupid, low-minded, and evil. In that way, country people earned a reputation (*villains*) they did not deserve.

# Lesson 5

"Better one living word than a hundred dead."

W.G. Benham, *Quotations*

1. **tradition** (tra dish′ ən) beliefs, opinions, and customs handed down from one generation to another
   a. The father tried to persuade* his son that the **tradition** of marriage was important.
   b. All religions have different beliefs and **traditions.**
   c. As time goes on, we will eliminate* **traditions** which are meaningless.

2. **rural** (rür′ əl) in the country
   a. Tomatoes are less expensive* at the **rural** farm stand.
   b. **Rural** areas are not densely* populated.
   c. The **rural** life is much more peaceful than the city one.

3. **burden** (bėr′ dən) what is carried; a load
   a. The **burden** of the country's safety is in the hands of the President.
   b. Irma found the enormous* box too much of a **burden.**
   c. Ricky carried the **burden** throughout his college career.

4. **campus** (kam′ pəs) grounds of a college, university, or school
   a. The **campus** was designed to utilize* all of the college's buildings.
   b. Jeff moved off **campus** when he decided it was cheaper to live at home.
   c. I chose to go to Penn State because it has a beautiful **campus.**

5. **majority** (mə jôr′ ə tē) the larger number; greater part; more than half
   a. A **majority** of votes was needed for the bill to pass.
   b. The **majority** of people prefer to pay wholesale* prices for meat.
   c. In some countries, the government does not speak for the **majority** of the people.

6. **assemble** (əs sem′ bl) gather together; bring together
   a. The rioters **assembled** outside the White House.
   b. I am going to **assemble** a model of a spacecraft.
   c. All the people who had **assembled** for the picnic vanished* when the rain began to fall.

7. **explore** (eks plôr′) go over carefully; look into closely; examine
   a. Lawyer Spence **explored** the essential* reasons for the crime.
   b. The Weather Bureau **explored** the effects of the rainy weather.
   c. Sara wanted to know if all of the methods for solving the problem had been **explored.**

8. **topic** (täp′ ik) subject that people think, write, or talk about
   a. Predicting* the weather is our favorite **topic** of conversation.
   b. Valerie only discussed **topics** that she knew well.
   c. The speaker's main **topic** was how to eliminate* hunger in this world.

9. **debate** (di bāt′) a discussion in which reasons for and against something are brought out
   a. The **debate** between the two candidates was heated.
   b. **Debate** in the U.S. Senate lasted for five days.
   c. Instead of shrieking* at each other, the students decided to have a **debate** on the topic.*

10. **evade** (i vād′) get away from by trickery or cleverness
    a. Juan tried to **evade** the topic* by changing the subject.
    b. In order to **evade** the draft, the young man had moved to Canada in 1968.
    c. The prisoner of war **evaded** questioning by pretending to be sick.

11. **probe** (prōb) search into; examine thoroughly; investigate
    a. The lawyer **probed** the man's mind to see if he was innocent.

b.   After **probing** the scientist's theory,* we proved it was correct.
c.   King Henry's actions were carefully **probed** by the noblemen.
12.   **reform** (ri fôrm′) make better; improve by removing faults
a.   After the prison riot, the council decided to **reform** the correctional system.
b.   Brad **reformed** when he saw that breaking the law was hurting people other than himself.
c.   Only laws that force companies to **reform** will clear the dangerous vapors* from our air.

---

*Read the following story to see how the new words are used in it.*

**Shape Up at Shaker**

Each summer at the Shaker Work Group, a special school in **rural** Pittsfield, Massachusetts, where teenagers learn by working, it has been a **tradition** to have the teenagers take on the **burden** of setting their own rules and living by them. Although there are some adults on the **campus**, teenagers are a **majority**.

One summer the group **assembled** to **explore** the **topic**: "lights-out time." There was little **debate** until 10:30 P.M. was suggested. Why? Everyone at the Shaker Work Group works a minimum* of several hours each morning on one project and several hours each afternoon on another. Since everyone has to get up early, no one wanted to stay up later at night anyway.

Few teenagers at the Shaker Work Group try to **evade** the rules. When one does, the entire group meets to **probe** the reasons for the "villain's"* actions. Their aim is to **reform** the rule breaker. However, at Shaker Village, the theory* is that teenagers who are busy working will have no time to break rules.

---

**Place one of the new words in each of the blanks below.**

1.   I left the city for a peaceful _____ farm.
2.   Professor Dixon liked the atmosphere of the university _____.
3.   He tried to _____ questions he didn't know how to answer.
4.   The _____ of people wanted him to be president.
5.   The guests began to _____ for Thanksgiving dinner.
6.   Christmas trees are a popular _____ for many people.
7.   Making a living for his family was too much of a _____.
8.   I want to _____ all the cities I haven't visited.
9.   If Gene doesn't _____, he will get into serious trouble.
10.   He had to do research on the _____ of biology for a school report.
11.   Historians will _____ the causes of the Vietnamese conflict.
12.   Whether or not eighteen year olds should be allowed to vote was in _____ for a long time.

---

**Exercise**
*Now make up your own sentences, one for each of the new words you have just been taught.*

1. _____
2. _____
3. _____
4. _____
5. _____
6. _____
7. _____

8. _____

9. _____

10. _____

11. _____

12. _____

**Spotlight on:**    **majority**—In recent years we have heard politicians talk about the "silent majority," meaning the average Americans who are decent persons, earn livings, follow the laws of the land, all in a quiet way. Those politicians might be surprised to learn that when the philosophers and writers of old used the term "silent majority" they were referring to dead people.

**Which of the words studied in this lesson is suggested by the picture?**

# Lesson 6

"A word to the wise is sufficient."

Plautus, *Persa*

1. **approach** (ə prōch′) come near or nearer to
   a. The lawyers were asked to **approach** the bench.
   b. Her beau* kissed Sylvia when he **approached** her.
   c. Ben **approached** the burden* of getting a job with a new spirit.

2. **detect** (di tekt′) find out; discover
   a. Sam Spade **detected** that the important papers had vanished.*
   b. From her voice it was easy to **detect** that Ellen was frightened.
   c. We **detected** from the messy room that a large group of people had assembled* there.

3. **defect** (di ′ fekt) fault; that which is wrong
   a. My Chevrolet was sent back to the factory because of a steering **defect.**
   b. His theory* of the formation of our world was filled with **defects.**
   c. The villain* was caught because his plan had many **defects.**

4. **employee** (em ploi ē′) a person who works for pay
   a. The **employees** went on strike for higher wages.
   b. My boss had to fire many **employees** when meat became scarce.*
   c. Joey wanted to go into business for himself and stop being an **employee.**

5. **neglect** (ni glekt′) give too little care or attention to
   a. The senator **neglected** to make his annual* report to Congress.
   b. Bob's car got dirty when he **neglected** to keep it polished.
   c. It is essential* that you do not **neglect** your homework.

6. **deceive** ( di sēv′) make someone believe as true something that is false; mislead
   a. Atlas was **deceived** about the burden* he had to carry.
   b. Virginia cried when she learned that her best friend had **deceived** her.
   c. The villain* **deceived** Chief White Cloud by pretending to be his friend.

7. **undoubtedly** (un dout′ id lē) certainly; beyond doubt
   a. Ray's team **undoubtedly** had the best debators* in our county.
   b. The pilgrims **undoubtedly** assembled* to travel to Rome together.
   c. If she didn't want to get into an argument, Valerie would have followed the majority* **undoubtedly.**

8. **popular** (pop′ ū lar) liked by most people
   a. The Beatles wrote many **popular** songs.
   b. At one time mini-skirts were very **popular.**
   c. **Popular** people often find it hard to evade* their many friends.

9. **thorough** (ther′ o) being all that is needed; complete
   a. The police made a **thorough** search of the house after the crime had been reported.
   b. My science teacher praised Sandy for doing a **thorough** job of cleaning up the lab.
   c. Mom decided to spend the day in giving the basement a **thorough** cleaning.

10. **client** (klī′ ənt) person for whom a lawyer acts; customer
    a. The lawyer told her **client** that she could predict* the outcome of his trial.
    b. My uncle tried to get General Motors to be a **client** of his company.
    c. If this restaurant doesn't improve its service, all its **clients** will vanish.*

11. **comprehensive** (käm′ pri hen′ siv) including much; covering completely
    a. After a **comprehensive** exam, my doctor said I was in good condition.

    b. The engineer gave our house a thorough*, **comprehensive** check-up before my father bought it.

    c. Mrs. Silver wanted us to do a **comprehensive** study of Edgar Allan Poe.

12. **defraud** (di frôd′) take money, rights, etc., away by cheating

    a. My aunt saved thousands of dollars by **defrauding** the government.

    b. If we could eliminate* losses from people who **defraud** the government, tax rates could be lowered.

    c. By **defrauding** his friend, Dexter ruined a family tradition* of honesty.

---

*Read the following story to see how the new words are used in it.*

### The Health of Your Car

The newest **approach** to automobile repair is the clinic, a place where car doctors go over an automobile in an attempt to **detect defects.** Since the clinic does no repairs, its **employees** do not **neglect** the truth. So many automobile owners feel that mechanics **deceive** them that the clinics, even though they **undoubtedly** charge high fees, are quite **popular.**

The experts do a **thorough** job for each **client.** They explore* every part of the engine, body, and brakes; they do all kinds of tests with expensive* machines. Best of all, the **comprehensive** examination takes only about half an hour. With the clinic's report in your hand no mechanic will be able to **defraud** you by telling you that you need major repairs when only a small repair is necessary.

---

**Which of the words studied in this lesson is suggested by the picture?**

**Place one of the new words in each of the blanks below.**

1. Each of our workers is trained to give your car a _____ examination. (Which *two* words might fit this sentence?)
2. Tom Jones was _____ the best singer in the choir when he was young.
3. He could _____ the problem from all angles.
4. Mrs. Spector always wanted to be _____ with her friends.
5. Why did you _____ cleaning your room today?
6. The _____ bought his boss a birthday present.
7. Rocco's only _____ was that he walked with a slight limp.
8. None of the other poker players suspected that their friend would _____ them in order to win.
9. When Cynthia realized that nobody liked her, she knew she had been _____.
10. I could _____ from the tone of his voice that he was in a bad mood.
11. His _____ was happy with the work Terence had been doing for him.
12. I do not want to do anything less than a _____ job on my term paper. (Which *two* words might fit this sentence?)

---

**Choose the Correct Word.** Circle the word in parentheses that best fits the sense of the sentence.

1. Many of today's (popular, comprehensive) songs will become tomorrow's Golden Oldies.
2. My boss insists that all of the (employees, clients) punch a time clock each morning.
3. I (approached, detected) a hint of sarcasm in your seemingly innocent reply to the sales clerk who apologized for the long lines.
4. As the car (approached, detected) the bridge, we could see the dense* fog coming in off the water.
5. Our weekly vocabulary quizzes are (comprehensive, popular), including not only that week's new words, but words we learned in past weeks as well.
6. Even a small (client, defect) in an electric appliance can be the possible* cause of a fire.
7. Ms. Rodriguez (undoubtedly, comprehensively) felt she had been unjustly accused of showing favoritism, but most of her students felt otherwise.
8. Her (thorough, popular) description of the missing bracelet helped police find it.
9. We've all learned that if you (defraud, neglect) your teeth, you will surely develop dental problems of one kind or another.
10. It is probably still true that the majority* of Americans do not think our political leaders would knowingly (defect, defraud) the government.
11. To (defraud, deceive) someone into thinking you are a friend when you are only along for the ride is selfish and unfeeling.
12. Since your livelihood depends on pleasing them, (clients, employees), like customers, are always right.

---

**Spotlight on:**   **defect**—Some of the new words have more than one part of speech—for example, they have meanings as verbs as well as nouns. *Defect* was defined for you as a noun: "fault; that which is wrong." It also serves as a verb, meaning "to quit a country, a political party, or a cause." One is said "to defect from Russia to the West" or "to defect from the Democratic Party." Which of the other words in Lesson 6 have more than one part of speech?

---

## Word Review #1

In the first six lessons you were taught 72 important words. The following exercises will test how well you learned some of those words.

**A.** In each of the parentheses below you will find two of the new vocabulary words. Pick the one that fits better. Remember, the sentence should make good sense.
1. It was a (dense, typical) day in July, hot and sticky.
2. I could tell that Matt was coming because I knew his (blend, vapor) of tobacco.
3. Please realize that if you try to climb the icy mountain (peril, tradition) awaits you.
4. The mechanic (defected, detected) an oil leak in the engine.
5. How could you (recline, neglect) paying the rent?
6. Felix made a (sinister, frigid) remark which sent chills up and down my spine.
7. Many questions had to be answered before Mrs. Soto could (qualify, evade) for the job.
8. I am (unaccustomed, dismal) to receiving gifts from people I don't know very well.
9. Factory-made goods are plentiful, but farm products are (rural, scarce).
10. When he got to the jail, the people in charge tried to (reform, abandon) him.

**B. Opposites.** In Column I are ten words which were taught in Lessons 1–6. Match them correctly with their *opposite* meanings, which you will find in Column II.

| Column I | Column II |
|---|---|
| 1. approach | a. unseen |
| 2. expensive | b. filled |
| 3. visible | c. hated |
| 4. popular | d. dull |
| 5. vacant | e. dry |
| 6. keen | f. be seen |
| 7. descend | g. leave |
| 8. humid | h. not needed |
| 9. vanish | i. climb |
| 10. essential | j. cheap |

**C.** Which of the vocabulary choices in parentheses fits best in these newspaper headlines?
1. **Sailors _____ Sinking Ship** (Defraud, Circulate, Abandon, Devise)
2. **Congress Votes To Raise _____ Wage** (Hardship, Minimum, Typical, Rural)
3. **_____ Fog Covers Bay Area** (Dense, Thorough, Scarce, Keen)
4. **Unfit Parents Arrested For Child _____** (Defect, Tradition, Neglect, Theory)
5. **Escaped Convict Continues To _____ Police** (Abandon, Evade, Inhabit, Conceal)
6. **College _____ Quiet After Demonstration** (Client, Campus, Debate, Probe)
7. **Mayor Takes _____ Of Office On Steps Of City Hall** (Oath, Data, Majority, Reform)
8. **Rescuers _____ Into Mine To Find Lost Workers** (Descend, Assemble, Circulate, Recline)
9. **New Apartment House To Rise On _____ Land** (Frigid, Comprehensive, Dense, Vacant)
10. **Poll To _____ Outcome Of Election** (Qualify, Predict, Tempt, Eliminate)

**D.** From the list of words below choose the word that means:
1. in large amounts *as well as* less costly
2. an evil doer *but originally meant* someone who lived on a farm
3. more than half *as well as* The legal age at which persons can manage their affairs
4. search or investigate *either* by means of an instrument or simply by questioning
5. cheat *and also* deprive someone of rights or property
6. give up on a plan *as well as* neglect one's post
7. gather (data) *or* just get together
8. reject *and also* expel
9. leaving out little or nothing *and* is related to the word for "understanding"
10. skill in dealing with people *as well as* a fine touch or cleverness

| deceive | tradition | abandon | persuade | inhabit | galant |
| thorough | evade | descend | comprehensive | eliminate | hardship |
| villain | assemble | circulate | beau | majority | wholesale |
| client | dense | predict | devise | defraud | recline |
| probe | theory | tact | conceal | data | tempt |

# Lesson 7

"A fool and his words are soon parted."

William Shenstone, *On Reserve*

**Words To Learn This Week**

postpone
consent
massive
capsule
preserve
denounce
unique
torrent
resent
molest
gloomy
unforeseen

1. **postpone** (pōst pōn′) put off to a later time; delay
   a. The young couple wanted to **postpone** their wedding until they were sure they could handle the burdens* of marriage.
   b. I neglected* to **postpone** the party because I thought everyone would be able to come.
   c. The supermarket's owner planned to **postpone** the grand opening until Saturday.

2. **consent** (kən sent′) agree; give permission or approval
   a. My teacher **consented** to let our class leave early.
   b. David would not **consent** to our plan.
   c. The majority* of our club members **consented** to raise the dues.

3. **massive** (mas′ iv) big and heavy; large and solid; bulky
   a. The boss asked some employees* to lift the **massive** box.
   b. From lifting weights, Willie had developed **massive** arm muscles.
   c. The main building on the campus* was so **massive** that the new students had trouble finding their way around at first.

4. **capsule** (kap′ səl) a small case or covering
   a. The small **capsule** contained notes the spy had written after the meeting.
   b. A new, untested medicine was detected* in the **capsule** by the police scientists.
   c. He explored* the space **capsule** for special equipment.

5. **preserve** (pri zėrv′) keep from harm or change; keep safe; protect
   a. The lawyers wanted to **preserve** the newest reforms* in the law.
   b. Farmers feel that their rural* homes should be **preserved.**
   c. Records of Hank Aaron's home runs will undoubtedly* be **preserved** in the Baseball Hall of Fame.

6. **denounce** (di nouns′) condemn in public; express strong disapproval of
   a. The father **denounced** his son for lying to the district attorney.
   b. Some people **denounce** the government for probing* into their private lives.
   c. Ralph Nader **denounced** the defective* products being sold.

7. **unique** (ū nēk′) having no like or equal; being the only one of its kind
   a. Going to Africa was a **unique** experience for us.
   b. The inventor developed a **unique** method of making ice cream.
   c. Albie has a **unique** collection of Israeli stamps.

8. **torrent** (tôr′ ənt) any violent, rushing stream; flood
   a. A massive* rain was coming down in **torrents.**
   b. In the debate, *a **torrent** of questions was asked.
   c. After trying to defraud* the public, Lefty was faced with a **torrent** of charges.

9. **resent** (ri zent′) feel injured and angered at (something)
   a. Bertha **resented** the way her boyfriend treated her.
   b. The earthquake victim **resented** the poor emergency care.
   c. Columbus **resented** the fact that his crew wanted to turn back.

10. **molest** (mə lest′) interfere with and trouble; disturb
    a. My neighbor was **molested** when walking home from the subway.
    b. The gang did a thorough* job of **molesting** the people in the park.
    c. Lifeguards warned the man not to **molest** any of the swimmers.

11. **gloomy** (glūm′ ē) dark; dim; in low spirits
    a. My cousin was **gloomy** because his best friend had moved away.
    b. The reason Doris wasn't popular* was that she always had a **gloomy** appearance.
    c. Jones Beach is not so beautiful on a **gloomy** day.
12. **unforeseen** (un fôr sēn′) not known beforehand; unexpected
    a. We had some **unforeseen** problems with the new engine.
    b. The probe* into the Congressman's finances turned up some **unforeseen** difficulties.
    c. The divers faced **unforeseen** trouble in their search for the wreck.

---

*Read the following story to see how the new words are used in it.*

### The Frozen Future

Doctors are always devising* new cures for diseases that kill people. But suppose you are dying from an incurable illness now. If only you could **postpone** death until a cure was found! Now some people are trying to do just that. One young man **consented** to having his body frozen and placed in a **massive capsule** in order to **preserve** it until doctors find a cure for his disease. Some people have **denounced** this **unique** experiment with a **torrent** of angry words. They **resent** human attempts to **molest** the natural order of life and death. There is also a **gloomy** fear that the world is already overcrowded and that people have to die to make room for those who are about to be born. If the experiment works, **unforeseen** problems undoubtedly* will arise.

---

**Which of the words studied in this lesson is suggested by the picture?**

**Place one of the new words in each of the blanks below.**

1. We have tried for over 200 years to _____ the United States Constitution.
2. The _____ weather predictions* upset him.
3. Will Karen _____ to having her baby picture published in the school newspaper?
4. I found a _____ collection of old books in the attic.
5. Dave knew that if he mistreated her, she would _____ it.
6. The President _____ the criminal activities that were going on.
7. Lori feared that if she walked the streets, she would be _____.
8. Owning a house created _____ difficulties.
9. The new movie invited a _____ of disapproval.
10. A telephone call told us that the employees'* picnic was _____ until next week.
11. The _____ was filled with records of the past.
12. It was a _____ job for just one person to unload the big truck.

---

**Exercise**

*Now make up your own sentences, one for each of the new words you have just been taught.*

1. _____
2. _____
3. _____
4. _____
5. _____
6. _____
7. _____
8. _____
9. _____
10. _____
11. _____
12. _____

---

**Spotlight on:**    **preserve**—Would you expect any connection between this word and *family?* Well, there is. In ancient times man was master of his household (*familia*) and the person who *served* him was the woman who had been captured and *preserved* from slaughter in order to work for the conqueror. In the 1500's a servant was called a *familiar.*

# Lesson 8

"By words the mind is excited and the spirit elated."

Aristophanes, *The Birds*

## Words To Learn This Week

exaggerate
amateur
mediocre
variety
valid
survive
weird
prominent
security
bulky
reluctant
obvious

1. **exaggerate** (eg zaj′ ər āt) make something greater than it is; overstate
   a. He wasn't trying to deceive* you when he said that his was the best car in the world; he was just **exaggerating.**
   b. The bookkeeper **exaggerated** her importance to the company.
   c. When he said that Kareem Abdul-Jabbar was eight feet tall, he was undoubtedly* **exaggerating.**

2. **amateur** (am′ e tə) person who does something for pleasure, not for money or as a profession
   a. The **amateur** cross-country runner wanted to be in the Olympics.
   b. After his song, Don was told that he wasn't good enough to be anything but an **amateur.**
   c. Professional golfers resent* **amateurs** who think they are as good as the people who play for money.

3. **mediocre** (mē di ō′ kər) neither good nor bad; average; ordinary
   a. After reading my composition, Mrs. Evans remarked that it was **mediocre** and that I could do better.
   b. Howard was a **mediocre** scientist who never made any unique* discoveries.
   c. The movie wasn't a great one; it was only **mediocre.**

4. **variety** (və rī′ ə tē) lack of sameness; a number of different things
   a. Eldorado Restaurant serves a wide **variety** of foods.
   b. The show featured a **variety** of entertainment.
   c. He faced unforeseen* problems for a **variety** of reasons.

5. **valid** (val′ id) supported by facts or authority; sound; true
   a. The witness neglected* to give **valid** answers to the judge's questions.
   b. Rita had **valid** reasons for denouncing* her father's way of life.
   c. When Dave presented **valid** working papers, the foreman consented* to hiring him immediately.

6. **survive** (sər vīv′) live longer than; remain alive after
   a. It was uncertain whether we would **survive** the torrent* of rain.
   b. Some people believe that only the strongest should **survive.**
   c. The space capsule* was built to **survive** a long journey in space.

7. **weird** (wêrd) mysterious; unearthly
   a. She looked **weird** with that horrible make-up on her face.
   b. Allen felt that **weird** things were starting to happen when he entered the haunted house.
   c. Becky had a **weird** feeling after swallowing the pills.

8. **prominent** (präm′ ə nənt) well-known; important
   a. My client* is a **prominent** businessperson.
   b. Charles DeGaulle is a **prominent** figure in the history of France.
   c. His big nose was the **prominent** feature of Jimmy Durante's face.

9. **security** (si kyur′ə tē) freedom from danger, care, or fear; feeling or condition of being safe
   a. Our janitor likes the **security** of having all doors locked at night.
   b. When the President travels, strict **security** measures are taken.
   c. Pablo wanted to preserve* the **security** of his life style.

10. **bulky** (bul′ kē) taking up much space; large
    a. Charley and Morty removed the **bulky** package from the car.
    b. The massive* desk was quite **bulky** and impossible to carry.
    c. His client* wanted an item that wasn't so **bulky,** Olsen told us.

11. **reluctant** (ri luk′ tənt) unwilling
    a.   It was easy to see that Herman was **reluctant** to go out and find a job.
    b.   The patient was **reluctant** to tell the nurse the whole gloomy* truth.
    c.   I was **reluctant** to give up the security* of family life.
12. **obvious** (ob′ vē əs) easily seen or understood; clear to the eye or mind; not to be doubted; plain
    a.   It was **obvious** that the lumberjack was tired after his day's work.
    b.   The fact that Darcy was a popular* boy was **obvious** to all.
    c.   The detective missed the clue because it was too **obvious.**

---

*Read the following story to see how the new words are used in it.*

### The Guitar

It is impossible to **exaggerate** the popularity* of the guitar. One out of every four **amateur** musicians in the United States plays the guitar. Even a **mediocre** player can produce a **variety** of music with this unique* instrument. Trying to find **valid** reasons for the guitar's ability to **survive** through the years isn't hard. One **weird** theory* by a **prominent** musician states that guitarists find **security** hiding behind the **bulky** instrument. But most people are **reluctant** to accept this idea because there are more **obvious** reasons for playing a guitar. It can be carried anywhere, it is inexpensive* to buy, and only a few lessons are required to learn to play it well.

---

**Which of the words studied in this lesson is suggested by the picture?**

**Place one of the new words in each of the blanks below.**

1. Most people agreed that he was a _____ looking man because of the long red beard.
2. Chuck's reason for quitting his job was _____; he was not being paid.
3. The answer to the question was so _____ that everyone knew it.
4. The _____ tennis player would never make the Olympic squad.
5. She was _____ to take on any more responsibilities at work.
6. People often tend to _____ stories they hear.
7. The bank is kept under very tight _____.
8. The big coat looked _____ on the midget.
9. Even though he was not a professional, the _____ photographer entered the contest.
10. A wide _____ of shows is playing at the concert hall.
11. Mrs. Meyers is a _____ member of the staff.
12. We all hoped that the small boat would _____ the storm.

---

**Matching.** Match the 12 new words in Column I with the definitions in Column II.

Column I

_____ 1. reluctant
_____ 2. mediocre
_____ 3. prominent
_____ 4. obvious
_____ 5. exaggerate
_____ 6. bulky
_____ 7. variety
_____ 8. valid
_____ 9. security
_____ 10. survive
_____ 11. weird
_____ 12. amateur

Column II

a. large; taking up much space
b. true; supported by facts
c. person who does something for pleasure, not as a profession
d. average; ordinary
e. mysterious; unearthly
f. unwilling
g. easily seen or understood
h. well-known; important
i. remain alive; live on
j. overstate; make something greater than it is
k. feeling or condition of being safe
l. a number of different things

---

**Spotlight on:**    **obvious**—Like so many of our words, this one comes from Latin roots—*ob* meaning "against" and *via* meaning "way." Something that met you on the way, therefore, was *obvious*. Look up the meanings of the Latin roots of some of the other words in Lesson 8 such as *exaggerate*, *survive*, and *prominent*.

# Lesson 9

"With words we govern men."

Benjamin Disraeli, *Contarini Fleming*

**Words To Learn
This Week**

vicinity
century
rage
document
conclude
undeniable
resist
lack
ignore
challenge
miniature
source

1. **vicinity** (və sin′ ə tē) region near a place; neighborhood
   a. Living in the **vicinity** of New York, Jeremy was near many museums.
   b. The torrent* of rain fell only in our **vicinity.**
   c. We approached* the Baltimore **vicinity** by car.

2. **century** (sen′ chə rē) 100 years
   a. George Washington lived in the eighteenth **century.**
   b. The United States is two **centuries** old.
   c. Many prominent* men have been born in this **century.**

3. **rage** (rāj) violent anger; something that arouses intense but brief enthusiasm
   a. Joan's bad manners sent her mother into a **rage.**
   b. In a fit of **rage,** Francine broke the valuable glass.
   c. The mayor felt a sense of **rage** about the exaggerations* in the press.

4. **document** (dok′ ū mənt) something handwritten or printed that gives information or proof of some fact
   a. Newly discovered **documents** showed that the prisoner was obviously* innocent.
   b. The **documents** of ancient Rome have survived* many centuries.*
   c. We were reluctant* to destroy important **documents.**

5. **conclude** (kən klōōd′) end; finish; decide
   a. Most people are happy when they **conclude** their work for the day.
   b. The gloomy* day **concluded** with a thunderstorm.
   c. Work on the building could not be **concluded** until the contract was signed.

6. **undeniable** (un di nī′ ə bəl) not to be denied; cannot be questioned
   a. The jury concluded* that the teenagers were **undeniably** guilty.
   b. It is **undeniable** that most professionals can beat any amateur.*
   c. That Leon resented* Rita's good marks in school was **undeniable.**

7. **resist** (rē zist′) act against; strive against; oppose
   a. Totie could not **resist** eating the chocolate sundae.
   b. Tight security* measures **resisted** Jimmy's entrance into the bank.
   c. Harold **resisted** the opportunity to poke fun at the weird* man.

8. **lack** (lak) be entirely without something; have not enough
   a. Your daily diet should not **lack** fruits and vegetables.
   b. His problem was that he **lacked** a variety* of talents.
   c. As an amateur* dancer, Vincent knew that he **lacked** the professional touch.

9. **ignore** (ig nôr′) pay no attention to; disregard
   a. Little Alice realized that if she didn't behave, her parents would **ignore** her.
   b. The student could not answer the question because he **ignored** the obvious* facts.
   c. Older brothers and sisters often feel **ignored** when their parents only spend time with a new baby.

10. **challenge** (chal′ ənj) call to a fight
    a. Aaron Burr **challenged** Alexander Hamilton to a duel.
    b. No one bothered to **challenge** the prominent* lawyer.
    c. Trying to become a doctor was quite a **challenge,** Dick discovered.

11. **miniature** (min′ ē ə tūr) represented on a small scale
    a. The young boy wanted a **miniature** sports car for his birthday.

b.  Instead of buying a massive* dog, Teddy got a **miniature** poodle.

c.  We were seeking a **miniature** model of the bulky* chess set.

12.  **source** (sôrs) place from which something comes or is obtained

a.  The college student knew that he needed more than a basic textbook as a **source** for his report.

b.  The **source** of Buddy's trouble was boredom.

c.  Professor Smith's speech was a valid* **source** of information on chemistry.

---

*Read the following story to see how the new words are used in it.*

## More About the Guitar

The guitar is one of the oldest instruments known to man. It probably originated in the **vicinity** of China. There were guitars in ancient Egypt and Greece as well, but the written history of the guitar starts in Spain in the 13th **century.** By 1500 the guitar was popular in Italy, France, and Spain. A French **document** of that time **concludes** that many people were playing the guitar. Stradivarius, the **undeniable** king of violin makers, could not **resist** creating a variety* of guitars. Also, there was no **lack** of music written for the instrument. Haydn, Schubert, and others wrote guitar music. When the great Beethoven was asked to compose music for the guitar, he went into a **rage** and refused, but eventually even Beethoven could not **ignore** the **challenge;** legend tells us he finally called the guitar a **miniature** orchestra. Indeed the guitar does sound like a little orchestra! Perhaps that is why in rural* areas around the world the guitar has been a **source** of music for millions to enjoy.

---

**Which of the words studied in this lesson is suggested by the picture?**

**Place one of the new words in each of the blanks below.**

1. Ernesto would constantly _____ his father's questions.
2. Historical _____ are kept in a special section of the library.
3. Great scientific progress has been made in this _____.
4. The massive* wrestler accepted the _____ of the newcomer.
5. Not wearing warm clothing was the _____ of his illness.
6. "When do you expect to _____ your investigation of the case?"
7. It is _____ that this restaurant's food is delicious.
8. Lena showed a _____ of good judgment.
9. Everyone who lived in the _____ of the bomb test was in peril.*
10. Anita's habit of interrupting him sent her husband into a _____.
11. My nephew was given a set of _____ soldiers for Christmas.
12. When you are tired it is hard to _____ staying in bed all day.

---

**Synonyms.** Circle the word that most nearly expresses the meaning of the word printed in heavy black type.

1. **century**   (a) countless years   (b) three score years   (c) one hundred years   (d) generation
2. **document**   (a) official paper   (b) critical review   (c) decree   (d) composition
3. **undeniable**   (a) essential*   (b) unforeseen*   (c) comprehensive   (d) unquestionable
4. **vicinity**   (a) region near a place   (b) division of a city or town   (c) residential district   (d) metropolitan area
5. **challenge**   (a) banish permanently   (b) verify easily   (c) call to a fight   (d) join together
6. **lack**   (a) take responsibility   (b) correct   (c) be without   (d) give freely
7. **miniature**   (a) balanced   (b) tiny   (c) eager   (d) forbidden
8. **rage**   (a) extreme anger   (b) foolish explanation   (c) rapid movement   (d) bad habit
9. **conclude**   (a) show   (b) reorganize   (c) examine   (d) decide
10. **source**   (a) origin   (b) task   (c) onlooker   (d) chart
11. **resist**   (a) discuss honestly   (b) change completely   (c) strive against   (d) pay attention
12. **ignore**   (a) disregard   (b) complete   (c) exaggerate*   (d) offer

---

**Spotlight on:**    century—In our slang, a "C-note" (*century*) stands for $100. Other slang references to money are "fin" ($5), "sawbuck" ($10), and "grand" ($1000). Look up the origins of these colorful terms for our dollars.

# Lesson 10

"Clearness is the most important matter in the use of words."

Quintillian, *De Institutione Oratoria*

## Words To Learn This Week

excel
feminine
mount
compete
dread
masculine
menace
tendency
underestimate
victorious
numerous
flexible

1. **excel** (ek sel') be better than; do better than
   a. Because he was so small, Larry could not **excel** in sports.
   b. At least Hannah had the security* of knowing that she **excelled** in swimming.
   c. Clarence Darrow wanted to become a prominent* lawyer, but he felt that he must first **excel** in history.

2. **feminine** (fem' ə nin) of women or girls
   a. When my sister wants to look **feminine** she changes from dungarees into a dress.
   b. Some men cannot resist* staring when they see a woman who is especially **feminine.**
   c. My brother is ashamed to cry at a sad movie because people might think he is behaving in a **feminine** manner.

3. **mount** (mount) get up on
   a. Senator Glenn **mounted** the platform to make his speech.
   b. The watchman **mounted** the tower to see if there were any people in the vicinity.*
   c. My sister couldn't **mount** the horse so they gave her a pony instead.

4. **compete** (kəm pēt') try hard to get something wanted by others; be a rival
   a. Pam Shriver was challenged* to **compete** for the tennis title.
   b. The runner was reluctant* to **compete** in front of his parents for the first time.
   c. When the amateur* became a pro he had to **compete** against better men.

5. **dread** (dred) look forward to with fear; fear greatly; causing great fear
   a. The poor student **dreaded** going to school each morning.
   b. He had a **dread** feeling about the challenge* he was about to face.
   c. I **dread** going into that deserted house.

6. **masculine** (mas' kū lin) of man; male
   a. The boy became more **masculine** as he got older.
   b. It is undeniable* that his beard makes him look **masculine.**
   c. The girls liked Jerry because of his **masculine** ways.

7. **menace** (men' is) threat
   a. Irv's lack* of respect made him a **menace** to his parents.
   b. The torrents* of rain were a **menace** to the farmer's crops.
   c. Sergeant Foy's raw language was an obvious* **menace** to the reputation of the entire police department.

8. **tendency** (ten' den sē) leaning; movement in a certain direction
   a. My algebra teacher has a **tendency** to forget the students' names.
   b. His **tendency** was to work hard in the morning and then to take it easy in the afternoon.
   c. The **tendency** in all human beings is to try to survive.*

9. **underestimate** (un dər es' tə māt) set too low a value, amount, or rate
   a. I admit that I **underestimated** the power in the bulky* fighter's frame.
   b. Undoubtedly* the boss **underestimated** his employee's* ability to work hard.
   c. The value of our house was **underestimated** by at least two thousand dollars.

10. **victorious** (vik tôʹ rē əs) having won a victory; conquering
    a. Playing in New Jersey, the Giants were **victorious** two years in a row.
    b. Terry faced the challenge* with the bad attitude that he could not be **victorious.**
    c. Our girls' volleyball squad was **victorious** over a taller team.

11. **numerous** (nooʹ mər əs) very many; several
    a. Critics review **numerous** movies every week.
    b. Dr. Fischer had resisted* accepting money from the poor woman on **numerous** housecalls.
    c. The debator* used **numerous** documents* to back up his statements.

12. **flexible** (flekʹ sə bəl) easily bent; willing to yield
    a. The toy was **flexible,** and the baby could bend it easily.
    b. Remaining **flexible,** Nick listened to arguments from both sides.
    c. A mouse's **flexible** body allows it to squeeze through narrow openings.

*Read the following story to see how the new words are used in it.*

### Bet on the Blonde

Can women **excel** as jockeys in big-time horse racing? Until recently the **feminine** touch was kept out of racing, but now at tracks all over the country women **mount** horses and **compete** with men, most of whom **dread** the whole idea. Their **masculine** image, they feel, may vanish.* Also, some offer the **weak** argument that females are a **menace** on the track. But, as we all know, we should resist* the **tendency** to **underestimate** the power of women. A few female jockeys have been **victorious** in **numerous** races, and this is probably what has put the male jockeys in a rage.* It would be wise if the men were more **flexible** in their attitudes toward women athletes.

### Place one of the new words in each of the blanks below.

1. The massive* tree on the corner was a _____ to traffic.
2. At parties, the shy girl would _____ being asked to dance.
3. My uncle has a _____ to repeat the same story over and over again.
4. The modest man used to _____ his own strength.
5. No person can ever _____ in all things he does.
6. Being _____ is far better than being stubborn.
7. We went to the beach on _____ occasions last summer.
8. Playing with dolls is traditionally* a _____ pastime, but attitudes are changing.
9. Only the brightest students were invited to _____ for the prize.
10. Carole was ten years old before her parents finally let her _____ a horse.
11. The amateur* tennis player completed many matches without being _____.
12. When Stuart started growing a mustache, it was obvious* he was becoming more _____.

### Exercise
*Now make up your own sentences, one for each of the new words you have just been taught.*

1. _____
2. _____
3. _____
4. _____
5. _____
6. _____
7. _____

8. _____

9. _____

10. _____

11. _____

12. _____

---

**Spotlight on:**    **mount**—A salesman of worthless goods and phoney remedies would often gather a crowd at a fair by juggling or doing some other lively antics. Sometimes he *mounted* a bench (bank) on which goods were displayed, and in that manner our English word *mountebank* came to mean a "quack" or a "fake."

---

**Which of the words studied in this lesson is suggested by the picture?**

# Lesson 11

*"We tie knots and bind up words in double meanings, and then try to untie them."*

Seneca, *Epistalae ad Lucilium*

1. **evidence** (ev′ ə dəns) that which makes clear the truth or falsehood of something
   a. Each juror felt he needed more **evidence** before voting to convict the accused killer.
   b. Her many awards were **evidence** enough that Leona excelled* in typing.
   c. Our teacher ignored* the **evidence** that Simon had cheated on the test.

2. **solitary** (säl′ ə ter ē) along; single; only
   a. Sid's **solitary** manner kept him from making new friendships.
   b. There was not a **solitary** piece of evidence* that Manuel had eaten the cheesecake.
   c. The convict went into a rage* when he was placed in a **solitary** cell.

3. **vision** (vizh′ ən) power of seeing; sense of sight
   a. With the aid of the binoculars, my **vision** improved enough to see the entire vicinity.*
   b. Ted Williams had perfect **vision,** and that helped to make him a great baseball player.
   c. The glasses which Irma bought corrected her near-sighted **vision.**

4. **frequent** (fre′ kwint) happening often; occurring repeatedly
   a. We made **frequent** visits to the hospital to see our grandfather.
   b. On **frequent** occasions Sam fell asleep in class.
   c. Dr. Bonner gave me some pills for my **frequent** headaches.

5. **glimpse** (glimps) a short, quick view
   a. This morning we caught our first **glimpse** of the beautiful shoreline.
   b. One **glimpse** of the very feminine* vision* was enough to tell Romeo that he loved Juliet.
   c. The tall shrubs kept us from getting a **glimpse** of the new people who inhabited* the beach house.

6. **recent** (rē′ sənt) done, made, or occurring not long ago
   a. At a **recent** meeting, the Board of Education provided the evidence* we had been asking for.
   b. Bessie liked the old silent movies better than the more **recent** ones.
   c. **Recent** studies have concluded* that more people are working than ever before.

7. **decade** (dek′ ād) ten years
   a. The 1960's was a **decade** of salary increases for employees.*
   b. Many people moved out of this city in the last **decade.**
   c. I have a vision* that this **decade** will be better than the last one.

8. **hesitate** (hez′ ə tāt) fail to act quickly; be undecided
   a. Nora **hesitated** to accept the challenge.*
   b. When he got to the robbers' vicinity,* he **hesitated** before going on.
   c. The proverb tells us that he who **hesitates** is lost.

9. **absurd** (ab sérd′) plainly not true or sensible; foolish
   a. It was **absurd** to believe the fisherman's tall tale.
   b. The flabby boy realized that the suggestion to diet was not **absurd.**
   c. Underestimating* the importance of reading is **absurd.**

10. **conflict** (kän′ flikt) direct opposition; disagreement
    a. Our opinions about the company's success in the last decade* are in **conflict** with what the records show.

    b.    There was a noisy **conflict** over who was the better tennis player.
    c.    The mayor and her assistant **conflict** in opinion frequently.*
11.    **minority** (mə nôr′ ə tē) smaller number or part; less than half
    a.    Only a small **minority** of the neighborhood didn't want a new park.
    b.    A **minority** of our athletes who competed* in the Olympics were victorious.*
    c.    Blacks are a **minority** group in the United States.
12.    **fiction** (fik′ shən) that which is imagined or made up
    a.    The story that the President had died was **fiction.**
    b.    We hardly ever believed Vinny because what he said was usually **fiction.**
    c.    Marge enjoys reading works of **fiction** rather than true stories.

---

*Read the following story to see how the new words are used in it.*

### The Famous Monster of the Lake

There seems to be more and more **evidence** that the enormous* monster in Loch Ness, a **solitary** lake in Scotland, is more than a **vision.** Each year there are numerous* **glimpses** of the monster by visitors and neighborhood people; also **recent** films, not easy to ignore,* are making even scientists **hesitate.** The story of **frequent** visits by a monster once seemed **absurd** to them but now they are not so sure.

Yet the **conflict** is far from over. Those who believe the monster exists are still in the **minority,** and they are constantly competing* for more information to prove that the Loch Ness monster is not a **fiction.** Even now they are trying to get more and clearer moving pictures of what has become the famous inhabitant* of the lake. Perhaps the question of whether the monster exists or not will be answered in this coming **decade.**

---

**Which of the words studied in this lesson is suggested by the picture?**

**Place one of the new words in each of the blanks below.**

1. The old man had lived for seven _____.
2. He had the _____ that some day there would be peace on earth.
3. Only a _____ of the senators were against welfare.
4. No one has ever had even a _____ of the future.
5. People used to think it was an _____ idea that human beings could ever fly.
6. We make _____ visits to Florida in the winter.
7. If you have any questions, don't _____ to ask.
8. There was only a _____ man on the beach.
9. The _____ was over the high cost of bread.
10. _____ studies have shown that the cost of living has gone up rapidly.
11. The gun alone was _____ enough to convict the killer.
12. The stories Henry told people about his adventures turned out to be merely _____.

---

**Matching.** Match the 12 new words in Column I with the definitions in Column II.

|  | Column I |  | Column II |
|---|---|---|---|
| _____ | 1. vision | a. | ten years |
| _____ | 2. fiction | b. | happening often |
| _____ | 3. frequent | c. | alone |
| _____ | 4. absurd | d. | that which makes clear the truth or falsehood of something |
| _____ | 5. minority | e. | occurring not long ago |
| _____ | 6. evidence | f. | a short, quick view |
| _____ | 7. conflict | g. | that which is imagined or made up |
| _____ | 8. decade | h. | sense of sight |
| _____ | 9. glimpse | i. | smaller number or part |
| _____ | 10. recent | j. | direct opposition |
| _____ | 11. solitary | k. | plainly not true or sensible |
| _____ | 12. hesitate | l. | fail to act quickly |

---

**Spotlight on:**    **absurd**—Here is another example of the ways in which original meanings changed through the centuries. At first, *absurd* meant "quite deaf." Its Latin roots also had the meanings of "out of tune, harsh, rough"—finally developing into "silly" or "senseless."

---

# Lesson 12

*"Sharp words make more wounds than surgeons can heal."*

Thomas Churchyard, *Mirror of Man*

## Words To Learn This Week

ignite
abolish
urban
population
frank
pollute
reveal
prohibit
urgent
adequate
decrease
audible

1. **ignite** (ig nīt′) set on fire
   a. Spark plugs **ignite** in an automobile engine.
   b. One match can **ignite** an entire forest.
   c. A careless remark helped to **ignite** the conflict* between the brothers and the sisters.

2. **abolish** (ə bäl′ ish) do away with completely; put an end to
   a. The death penalty has recently* been **abolished** in our state.
   b. We **abolished** numerous* laws which didn't serve any purpose in this decade.*
   c. My school has **abolished** final exams altogether.

3. **urban** (ėr′bən) of or having to do with cities or towns
   a. Many businesses open offices in **urban** areas.
   b. I plan to exchange my **urban** location for a rural* one.
   c. Only a small minority* of the people of the United States live far from any **urban** area.

4. **population** (pop ū lā shən) people of a city or country
   a. China has the largest **population** of any country.
   b. The **population** of the world has increased in every decade.*
   c. After the recent* floods, the **population** of Honduras was reduced by 10,000.

5. **frank** (frangk) free in expressing one's real thoughts, opinions, or feelings; not hiding what is in one's mind
   a. Never underestimate* the value of being **frank** with one another.
   b. Eretha was completely **frank** when she told her friend about the sale.
   c. People liked Duffy because they knew he would be **frank** with them.

6. **pollute** (pə lōot′) make dirty
   a. The Atlantic Ocean is in danger of becoming **polluted.**
   b. There is much evidence* to show that the air we breathe is **polluted.**
   c. It is claimed that soap powders **pollute** the water we drink.

7. **reveal** (ri vēl′) make known
   a. Napoleon agreed to **reveal** the information to the French population.*
   b. The evidence* was **revealed** only after hours of questioning.
   c. General Motors **revealed** reluctantly* that there were defects* in their new Buicks.

8. **prohibit** (prō′ hib′ it) forbid by law or authority
   a. Elvin's manager **prohibited** him from appearing on television.
   b. Many homeowners **prohibit** others from walking on their property.
   c. The law **prohibits** the use of guns to settle a conflict.*

9. **urgent** (ėr′ jənt) demanding immediate action or attention; important
   a. An **urgent** telephone call was made to the company's treasurer.
   b. The principal called an **urgent** meeting to solve the school's numerous* problems.
   c. When he heard the **urgent** cry for help, the lifeguard did not hesitate.*

10. **adequate** (ad′ ə kwit) as much as is needed; fully sufficient
    a. Rover was given an **adequate** amount of food to last him the whole day.
    b. A bedroom, kitchen, and bath were **adequate** shelter for his living needs.
    c. Carlos was **adequate** at his job but he wasn't great.

11. **decrease** (di krēs′) make or become less
    a. As he kept spending money, the amount he saved **decreased.**
    b. In order to improve business, the store owner **decreased** his prices.
    c. The landlord promised to **decrease** our rent.

35

12. **audible** (ô də bəl) able to be heard
   a.  From across the room, the teacher's voice was barely **audible**.
   b.  After Len got his new hearing aid, my telephone calls became **audible**.
   c.  Commands from Ann's drill sergeant were always easily **audible**.

*Read the following story to see how the new words are used in it.*

### The Electric Auto Is on Its Way

**Ignite** gasoline and you have noise and smoke; turn on an electric motor and you **abolish** two headaches which are dreaded* by **urban populations.** Automobile manufacturers are **frank** about the way their motors **pollute** the air, and that is why there are frequent* hints that the big companies will soon **reveal** a model electric car.

So far, lack* of knowledge in storing electricity in the car **prohibits** wide production of electric autos, but recently* Congress called **urgently** for **adequate** research into the battery or fuel cell problem. Electric autos would be inexpensive* to run and would **decrease** air pollution.* It might be weird,* however, to live in the quiet surroundings of a city where autos which used to be noisily **audible** would be whisper-quiet.

**Which of the words studied in this lesson is suggested by the picture?**

**Place one of the new words in each of the blanks below.**

1. The doctor was completely _____ with the dying man.
2. In an _____ whisper, Maria called for my attention.
3. We didn't need any evidence* to see that the poor man was in _____ need of money and food.
4. All his life the child was used to living in _____ areas.
5. Dry matches to _____ the campfire were sought by the boy scout.
6. Smoking is _____ in the medical building.
7. Gasoline fumes help to _____ the air.
8. The_____in the number of people voting in national elections is due to lack* of interest.
9. Some citizens believe that we will never be able to _____ war.
10. The_____of New York City is about seven million people.
11. In the comics, Superman never _____ his true identity.
12. They needed an _____ supply of water to last for the entire trip through the desert.

---

**Which Word Means.** From the list of 12 new words that follows, choose the one that corresponds to each definition below.

| | | | |
|---|---|---|---|
| ignite | abolish | urban | population |
| frank | pollute | reveal | prohibit |
| urgent | adequate | decrease | audible |

1. having to do with cities or towns _____
2. make known _____
3. as much as is needed; sufficient _____
4. make dirty _____
5. do away with completely _____
6. make or become less _____
7. free in expressing one's thoughts _____
8. demanding immediate action _____
9. set on fire _____
10. people of a city or country _____
11. able to be heard _____
12. forbid by law or authority _____

---

**Spotlight on:    ignite**—In 1973–1974 much attention was given to the fiery comet Kohoutek which was supposed to blaze spectacularly across the sky. The people of medieval times spoke of four such types of natural history: *aerial meteors* (winds), *aqueous meteors* (rain, snow), *luminous meteors (rainbow, halo)* and *igneous meteors* (lightning, shooting stars). Now that you know the definition of *ignite*, you can see why such heavenly occurrences were called *igneous*.

# Word Review #2

Here are some of the words which were covered in Lessons 7–12. The following exercises will test how well you learned them.

**A.** In each of the parentheses below you will find two of the new vocabulary words. Choose the one that fits better.

1. We will have to (postpone, decrease) our meeting unless more members show up.
2. Rex (underestimated, resisted) the skill of the other tennis player, and he was beaten badly.
3. With only a (frank, mediocre) typing ability, Veronica never expected to be hired.
4. Germs are a (menace, dread) to our health.
5. Although Rip was (challenged, reluctant) to tell all he knew, he remained silent.
6. We invited only the most (prominent, undeniable) people in town to our fund-raising party.
7. When her job in the city was (molested, abolished), Daisy went home to the farm.
8. (Unforeseen, Amateur) problems kept coming up each day, making it harder and harder for me to finish my work.
9. I believe in our doctor and like the (absurd, adequate) reasons he gave us for keeping Grandma in the hospital.
10. Don't you get angry when someone (ignores, concludes) your questions?

**B. Opposites.** In Column I are ten words which were taught in Lessons 7–12. Match them correctly with their *opposite* meanings, which you will find in Column II.

| Column I | Column II |
|---|---|
| 1. consent | a. put out |
| 2. valid | b. not important |
| 3. ignite | c. die |
| 4. reveal | d. refuse |
| 5. urgent | e. allow |
| 6. victorious | f. large |
| 7. survive | g. get off |
| 8. mount | h. hide |
| 9. prohibit | i. beaten |
| 10. miniature | j. untrue |

**C.** Which of the vocabulary choices in parentheses fits best in these newspaper headlines?

1. "Charges Against Me Are ____," Complains Governor    (Undeniable, Frank, Absurd, Mediocre)
2. High School Principal To _____ Student Autos    (Preserve, Prohibit, Abolish, Underestimate)
3. _____ Flight Of Space Ship For 48 Hours    (Unforeseen, Ignite, Preserve, Postpone)
4. Witness Promises To _____ Truth Today    (Reveal, Denounce, Exaggerate, Challenge)
5. "Best Novel In A _____," Says Critic    (Conflict, Decade, Variety, Fiction)
6. Sick Child Visited By _____ Specialist    (Obvious, Prominent, Amateur, Dread)
7. Flu Germs _____ Elderly Citizens    (Menace, Resist, Pollute, Prohibit)
8. Stolen Jewels Are Objects Of _____ Search    (Adequate, Valid, Unforeseen, Massive)
9. Huge Unemployment In _____ Areas    (Reluctant, Recent, Urban, Urgent)
10. Weatherman Apologizes For _____ Weekend Forecast    (Valid, Gloomy, Obvious, Solitary)

**D.** From the list of words below choose the word that means:

1. be undecided *as well as* show reluctance
2. an untruth *but* one that is practiced by even the best writers
3. ponderous or large *and* is the opposite of *capsule*
4. ten decades *and* has the same root as *cent*
5. finish *as well as* make an inference
6. ridiculous *yet in a certain phrase* is close to *sublime*
7. *easily understood as well as* evident and apparent
8. save *and in its origin* bears a relation to *family*
9. a dream or hope *as well as* sight
10. one of a kind *and also* rare or without equal

| | | | | | |
|---|---|---|---|---|---|
| conclude | solitary | excel | massive | fiction | preserve |
| urban | obvious | menace | denounce | vision | century |
| torrent | unique | compete | tendency | security | source |
| frank | glimpse | dread | numerous | mediocre | undeniable |
| decrease | conflict | hesitate | document | reluctant | absurd |

# Lesson 13

"He can compress the most words into the smallest ideas of any man I ever met."

Abraham Lincoln, of a fellow lawyer

**Words To Learn This Week**

journalist
famine
revive
commence
observant
identify
migrate
vessel
persist
hazy
gleam
editor

1. **journalist** (jėr′ nəl ist) one who writes for, edits, manages, or produces a newspaper or magazine
   a. There were four **journalists** covering the murder story.
   b. Barbara's experience working at a book store wasn't adequate* preparation for becoming a **journalist.**
   c. A **journalist** must have a comprehensive* knowledge* of the city where he or she works.

2. **famine** (fam′ ən) starvation; great shortage
   a. **Famine** in India caused the death of one-tenth of the population.*
   b. There has been a **famine** of good writing in the last decade.*
   c. The rumor of a **famine** in Europe was purely fiction.*

3. **revive** (ri vīv′) bring back or come back to life or consciousness
   a. There is a movement to **revive** old plays for modern audiences.
   b. The nurses tried to **revive** the heart attack victim.
   c. Committees are trying to **revive** interest in population* control.

4. **commence** (kə mens′) begin; start
   a. Graduation will **commence** at ten o'clock.
   b. Bella hesitated* before **commencing** her speech.
   c. The discussion **commenced** with a report on urban* affairs.

5. **observant** (ab zer′ vənt) quick to notice; watchful
   a. We were **observant** of the conflict* between the husband and his wife.
   b. Because Cato was **observant,** he was able to reveal* the thief's name.
   c. Milt used his excellent vision* to be **observant** of everything in his vicinity.*

6. **identify** (ī den′ tə fī) recognize as being, or show to be, a certain person or thing; prove to be the same
   a. Numerous* witnesses **identified** the butcher as the killer.
   b. Mrs. Shaw was able to **identify** the painting as being hers.
   c. With only a quick glimpse,* Reggie was able to **identify** his girlfriend in the crowd.

7. **migrate** (mī′ grāt) move from one place to another
   a. The fruit pickers **migrated** to wherever they could find work.
   b. Much of our population* is constantly **migrating** to other areas of the country.
   c. My grandfather **migrated** to New York from Italy in 1919.

8. **vessel** (ves′ əl) a ship; a hollow container; tube containing body fluid
   a. The Girl Scouts were permitted a glimpse* of the **vessel** being built when they toured the Navy Yard.
   b. My father burst a blood **vessel** when he got the bill from the garage.
   c. Congress voted to decrease* the amount of money being spent on space **vessels.**

9. **persist** (pər sist′) continue firmly; refuse to stop or be changed
   a. The humid* weather **persisted** all summer.
   b. Would Lorraine's weird* behavior **persist,** we all wondered?
   c. Lloyd **persisted** in exaggerating* everything he said.

10. **hazy** (hā′ zē) misty; smoky; unclear
    a. The vicinity* of London is known to be **hazy.**
    b. Factories that pollute* the air create **hazy** weather conditions.
    c. Although Cora had a great memory, she was unusually **hazy** about the details of our meeting on January 16th.

11. **gleam** (glēm) a flash or beam of light
    a.  A **gleam** of light shone through the prison window.
    b.  The only source* of light in the cellar came in the form of a **gleam** through a hole in the wall.
    c.  My grandmother gets a **gleam** in her eyes when she sees the twins.

12. **editor** (ed′ ə tər) person who prepares a publication; one who corrects a manuscript and helps to improve it
    a.  The student was proud to be the **editor** of the school newspaper.
    b.  Meredith's journalistic knowledge* came in handy when he was unexpectedly given the job of **editor** of The Bulletin.
    c.  It is undeniable* that the magazine has gotten better since Ellis became **editor.**

*Read the following story to see how the new words are used in it.*

**Flying Saucers Again**

Whenever **journalists** face a news **famine** they **revive** the undeniably* interesting question: How can we explain UFO's—unidentified flying objects? The story usually **commences** with a description of the object by some **observant** night watchman who doesn't hesitate* to **identify** the object as having **migrated** from outer space. The **vessel,** he **persists,** appeared over the **hazy** lake at about 30 feet. A greenish **gleam** prohibited* him from seeing its exact shape, he admits. Newspaper **editors** love these stories because they keep the population* interested in knowledge  about UFO's and keep them buying newspapers.

**Place one of the new words in each of the blanks below.**

1.  The wedding will _____ at eight o'clock.
2.  When Abe lost his job, he had to _____ to a place where he could find work.
3.  We could tell Ira was happy by the bright _____ in his eyes.
4.  Because of the _____, people were dying in the streets.
5.  Many people claim to have seen a ghostly _____ sailing through the fog.
6.  Can you _____ the flags of all the states in the United States?
7.  He was _____ of all the rules of his religion.
8.  The _____ sent five reporters to cover the big story.
9.  They were trying to _____ interest in old movies.
10. The travelers were stupid to _____ in eating the food after they were told it was spoiled.
11. _____weather kept the pilot from seeing the airfield clearly.
12. The young _____ applied for his first job at a small newspaper.

**Exercise**
*Now make up your own sentences, one for each of the new words you have just been taught.*

1. _____
2. _____
3. _____
4. _____
5. _____

6. _____

7. _____

8. _____

9. _____

10. _____

11. _____

12. _____

**Which of the words studied in this lesson is suggested by the picture?**

**Spotlight on:**    **commence**—Many people have wondered why the end of someone's school days should be celebrated by *Commencement* Exercises which, ordinarily, refer to a beginning. The reason for that term is that we often think of the completion of an education as the time to *commence* or begin to earn a livelihood.

# Lesson 14

"Words, like fine flowers, have their colors, too."

Ernest Rhys, *Words*

**Words To Learn
This Week**

unruly
rival
violent
brutal
opponent
brawl
duplicate
vicious
whirling
underdog
thrust
bewildered

1. **unruly** (un r$\overline{oo}$' lē) hard to rule or control; lawless
   a. **Unruly** behavior is prohibited* at the pool.
   b. When he persisted* in acting **unruly,** Ralph was fired from his job.
   c. His **unruly** actions were a menace* to those who were trying to work.

2. **rival** (rī' vəl) person who wants and tries to get the same thing as another; one who tries to equal or do better than another
   a. The boxer devised* an attack which would help him to be victorious* over his young **rival.**
   b. Sherry didn't like to compete* because she always thought her **rival** would win.
   c. Seidman and Son decided to migrate* to an area where they would have fewer **rivals.**

3. **violent** (vī' ə lənt) acting or done with strong, rough force
   a. Carefully, very carefully, we approached* the **violent** man.
   b. **Violent** behavior is prohibited* on school grounds.
   c. Vernon had a tendency* to be **violent** when someone angered him.

4. **brutal** (br$\overline{oo}$' təl) coarse and savage; like a brute; cruel
   a. Dozens of employees* quit the job because the boss was **brutal** to them.
   b. The **brutal** track coach persisted* in making the team work out all morning under the hot sun.
   c. Swearing to catch the murderer, the detectives revealed* that it had been an unusually **brutal,** violent* crime.

5. **opponent** (ə pō' nənt) person who is on the other side of a fight, game, or discussion; person fighting, struggling or speaking against another
   a. The Russian chess player underestimated* his **opponent** and lost.
   b. He was a bitter **opponent** of costly urban* reform.
   c. Seeing his flabby* **opponent,** Slugger was sure he would be victorious.*

6. **brawl** (brôl) a noisy quarrel or fight
   a. The journalist* covered all the details of the **brawl** in the park.
   b. Larry dreaded* a **brawl** with his father over finding a job.
   c. What started out as a polite discussion soon became a violent* **brawl.**

7. **duplicate** (d$\overline{oo}$' plə kāt) an exact copy; make an exact copy of; repeat exactly
   a. Elliott tried to deceive* Mrs. Held by making a **duplicate** of my paper.
   b. We **duplicated** the document* so that everyone had a copy to study.
   c. The so-called expert did a mediocre* job of **duplicating** the Van Gogh painting.

8. **vicious** (vish' əs) evil; wicked; savage
   a. Liza was unpopular* because she was **vicious** to people she had just met.
   b. The **vicious** editor* published false stories about people he disliked.
   c. Mr. Voss was reluctant* to talk about his **vicious** St. Bernard dog.

9. **whirling** (hwər' ling) turning or swinging round and round; spinning
   a. The space vessel* was **whirling** around before it landed on earth.
   b. As they tried to lift the bulky* piano, the movers went **whirling** across the living room.
   c. Because Angelo drank too much, he commenced* to feel that everything was **whirling** around the bar.

10. **underdog** (un' dər dôg) person having the worst of any struggle; one who is expected to lose
    a. Minority* groups complain about being the **underdogs** in this century.*

    b.   I always feel sorry for the **underdog** in a street fight.

    c.   The Jets were identified* as **underdogs** even though they had beaten the Los Angeles Rams earlier in the season.

11.   **thrust** (thrust) push with force

    a.   Once the jet engine was ignited,* it **thrust** the rocket from the ground.

    b.   He had adequate* strength to **thrust** himself through the locked door.

    c.   Eva was in a terrible rage* when she **thrust** herself into the room.

12.   **bewildered** (bi wil′ dėrd) confused completely; puzzled

    a.   The lawyer was **bewildered** by his client's* lack* of interest in the case.

    b.   His partner's weird* actions left Jack **bewildered.**

    c.   **Bewildered** by the sudden hazy* weather, he decided not to go to the beach.

---

*Read the following story to see how the new words are used in it.*

### Roller Derby

The most **unruly** game known to man or woman is the Roller Derby. Revived* every so often on television, it has no **rival** for **violent, brutal** action. The game commences* with two teams on roller skates circling a banked, oval track. Then one or two skaters try to break out of the pack and "lap" the **opponents.** When the skater leaves the pack, the **brawl** begins. No sport can duplicate the **vicious** shrieking,* pushing, elbowing, and fighting all at high speed while the skaters are **whirling** around the track. And women are just as much of a menace* as the men. Often considered the **underdog,** the female skater can **thrust** a pointed fingernail into the face of a **bewildered** enemy.

---

**Which of the words studied in this lesson is suggested by the picture?**

**Place one of the new words in each of the blanks below.**

1. Rory was thrown out of school because of his _____ behavior.
2. The _____ lion attacked the lost child in the forest.
3. They had a _____ over who was a better swimmer.
4. The magician _____ his hand into his hat, and out came a rabbit.
5. A man was caught trying to _____ documents* that were top secret.
6. His _____ was a man who was trying to win the heart of his girl.
7. The experienced chess player tried to keep his _____ guessing.
8. The boy was_____by the fact that his parents had abandoned* him.
9. Whenever the skinny boy got into a fight he was the _____.
10. When some animals aren't fed on time they become very _____.
11. The ball was hit so hard that it went _____ down the field.
12. Five hundred men were killed in that _____ battle.

(NOTE: The same words could be used in Sentences 2, 10, and 12; similarly, you may have a problem in deciding about the proper words to use in Sentences 6 and 7.)

---

**True or False.** Based on the way the new word is used, write T(true) or F (false) next to the sentence.

_____ 1. A **violent** person is someone who uses strong, rough force.
_____ 2. An **underdog** is someone who is likely to win.
_____ 3. A **brawl** is a noisy quarrel or fight.
_____ 4. To **thrust** means to push forcibly.
_____ 5. A **rival** is someone who wants and tries to get the same thing as another.
_____ 6. **Unruly** means easy to control.
_____ 7. **Brutal** means sweet-tempered and easygoing.
_____ 8. An **opponent** is a person or group who is on the other side of a fight, game, or discussion.
_____ 9. A **duplicate** is something that is imagined or made up.
_____10. To be **bewildered** is to be ready for action.
_____11. A **vicious** act is one that is evil, wicked, and savage.
_____12. **Whirling** means turning or swinging round and round.

---

**Spotlight on:** rival—Probably comes from the Latin *rivus* (stream). Those who lived on the opposite banks of a river were likely to be *rivals*. Today, in big cities, it is likely to be a matter of *turf* (neighborhood streets) over which *rival* gangs sometimes fight.

# Lesson 15

"Speak clearly, if you speak at all;
Carve every word before you let it fall."

Oliver Wendell Holmes, *A Rhymed Lesson*

**Words To Learn
This Week**

expand
alter
mature
sacred
revise
pledge
casual
pursue
unanimous
fortunate
pioneer
innovative

1. **expand** (i k spand′) increase in size; enlarge; swell
   a. We will **expand** our business as soon as we locate a new building.
   b. Present laws against people who pollute* the air must be **expanded.**
   c. **Expanding** the comic strips, the editor* hoped that more people would buy his paper.

2. **alter** (ôl′ tər) make different; change; vary
   a. I **altered** my typical* lunch and had a steak instead.
   b. Dorothy agreed to **alter** my dress if I would reveal* its cost to her.
   c. It's absurd* to spend money to **alter** that old candy store.

3. **mature** (mə choor′ or mətur′) ripe; fully grown or developed
   a. I could tell that Mitch was **mature** from the way he persisted* in his work.
   b. Only through **mature** study habits can a person hope to gain knowledge.*
   c. It is essential* that you behave in a **mature** way in the business world.

4. **sacred** (sā′ krid) worthy of respect; holy
   a. Her **sacred** medal had to be sold because the family was in urgent* need of money.
   b. It was revealed* by the journalist* that the **sacred** temple had been torn down.
   c. Kate made a **sacred** promise to her parents never to miss a Sunday church service.

5. **revise** (ri vīz′) change; alter*; bring up to date
   a. My family **revised** its weekend plans when the weather turned hazy.*
   b. The dictionary was **revised** and then published in a more expensive* edition.
   c. Under the **revised** rules, Shane was eliminated* from competing.*

6. **pledge** (plej) promise
   a. Before the grand jury, the sinister* gangster **pledged** to tell the whole truth.
   b. Monte was reluctant* to **pledge** his loyalty* to his new girlfriend.
   c. **Pledged** to discovering the facts, the journalist* began to dig up new evidence* for his readers.

7. **casual** (kazh′ ū əl) happening by chance; not planned or expected; not calling attention to itself
   a. As the villain* stole the money from the blind man, he walked away in a **casual** manner.
   b. The bartender made a **casual** remark about the brawl* in the backroom.
   c. Following a **casual** meeting on the street, the bachelor* renewed his friendship with the widow.

8. **pursue** (pər soo′) follow; proceed along
   a. We **pursued** the bicycle thief until he vanished* from our vision.*
   b. Ernie rowed up the river, **pursuing** it to its source.*
   c. The senior wanted to **pursue** urban* affairs as his life's work.

9. **unanimous** (yu̇ nan′ ə məs) in complete agreement
   a. The class was **unanimous** in wanting to eliminate* study halls.
   b. There has never been an election in our union which was won by a **unanimous** vote.
   c. The Senate, by a **unanimous** vote, decided to decrease* taxes.

10. **fortunate** (fôr′ chə nit) having good luck; lucky
    a. Wesley was **fortunate** to have an adequate* sum of money in the bank.
    b. It is **fortunate** that the famine* did not affect our village.
    c. The underdog* was **fortunate** enough to come out a winner.

11. **pioneer** (pī ə nēr′) one who goes first or prepares a way for others
    a. My grandfather was a **pioneer** in selling wholesale* products.
    b. England was a **pioneer** in building large vessels* for tourists.
    c. In the fourth grade I assembled* a picture collection of great American **pioneers.**

12. **innovative** (ine vā′ tiv) fresh; clever; having new ideas
    a. The **innovative** ads for the candy won many new customers.
    b. Everyone in our office praised the boss for his **innovative** suggestions.
    c. Nicole decided to alter* her approach and become more **innovative.**

*Read the following story to see how the new words are used in it.*

## John Dewey High School; Brooklyn, New York

The high school of the future may be New York City's John Dewey High School. Located in Brooklyn, this unique* school offers an **expanded, altered** course of study for **mature** students. The **sacred** 40 minute period has been abolished* and replaced with 20 minute units, so that some classes are 20, 40, 60 or even 80 minutes long. Courses have been **revised** into seven-week units. In honor study halls, students **pledge** themselves to quiet study. Gener-ally, the teachers' attitude towards students is **casual.** Pupils may utilize* the cafeteria any time they have no class. Pupils **pursue** courses they choose themselves. So far the positive reaction is **unanimous;** everyone senses that the **fortunate** students at John Dewey High School are **pioneers** in the thrust* to find new ways of teaching and learning. We salute this **innovative** school.

**Place one of the new words in each of the blanks below.**

1. Dominick was _____ to have such good friends.
2. Rhonda didn't believe in divorce because she felt that marriage is _____.
3. The pilot had to _____ his course when he ran into bad weather.
4. Everyone approved of Dave's _____ proposal.*
5. David wanted to _____ medicine as a career.
6. He moved out of the house when he became a _____ young man.
7. The vote to make Jim president of the camera club was _____.
8. When his mother died of cancer, the young doctor decided to _____ his life to finding a cure for it.
9. They had to _____ their plans when a third person decided to join them for lunch.
10. The young people that went to Woodstock were the _____ of the outdoor rock music festival.
11. The relaxed friends spoke in a _____ manner as they talked on the street.
12. I can feel my stomach _____ when I breathe deeply.

## Exercise

*Now make up your own sentences, one for each of the new words you have just been taught.*

1. _____
2. _____
3. _____
4. _____
5. _____

6. _____

7. _____

8. _____

9. _____

10. _____

11. _____

12. _____

**Spotlight on:** **pioneer**—Originally derived from an old French word for a foot soldier, *peonier*, the word has come to mean much more than the first to settle a region. It now also refers to those who open new fields of inquiry, even new worlds. Thus, we have space pioneers and pioneers in cancer research. Ecologists, who deal with the adaptation of life to the environment, even call a plant or animal which successfully invades and becomes established in a bare area a pioneer.

**Which of the words studied in this lesson is suggested by the picture?**

# Lesson 16

"A very great part of the mischiefs that vex this world arises from words."

Edmund Burke, *Letters*

**Words To Learn This Week**

slender
surpass
vast
doubt
capacity
penetrate
pierce
accurate
microscope
grateful
cautious
confident

1. **slender** (slen' dər) long and thin; limited; slight
   a. Carlotta's **slender** figure made her look very feminine.*
   b. There was only a **slender** chance that you could conceal* the truth.
   c. The **slender** thief was able to enter the apartment through the narrow window.

2. **surpass** (sər pas') do better than; be greater than; excel*
   a. The machines of the twentieth century* surely **surpass** those of earlier times.
   b. Most farmers believe that rural* life far **surpasses** urban* living.
   c. It is undeniable* that a cold lemonade in July cannot be **surpassed.**

3. **vast** (vast) very great; enormous*
   a. Daniel Boone explored* **vast** areas that had never been settled.
   b. Our campus* always seems **vast** to new students.
   c. **Vast** differences between the two sides were made clear in the debate.*

4. **doubt** (dout) not believe; not be sure of; feel uncertain about; lack of certainty
   a. Scientists **doubt** that a total cure for cancer will be found soon.
   b. The question of whether he could survive* the winter was left in **doubt.**
   c. We don't **doubt** that the tradition* of marriage will continue.

5. **capacity** (kə pas' ə tē) amount of room or space inside; largest amount that can be held by a container
   a. A sign in the elevator stated that its **capacity** was 1100 pounds.
   b. The gasoline capsule* had a **capacity** of 500 gallons.
   c. So well-liked was the prominent* speaker that the auditorium was filled to **capacity** when he began his lecture.

6. **penetrate** (pen' ə trāt) get into or through
   a. We had to **penetrate** the massive* wall in order to hang the mirror.
   b. Although Kenny tried to pound the nail into the rock with a hammer, he couldn't **penetrate** the hard surface.
   c. The thieves **penetrated** the bank's security* and stole the money.

7. **pierce** (pērs) go into; go through; penetrate*
   a. My sister is debating* whether or not to get her ears **pierced.**
   b. I tried to ignore* his bad violin playing, but the sound was **piercing.**
   c. Halloran violently* **pierced** the skin of his rival,* causing massive* bleeding.

8. **accurate** (ak' ū rit) exactly right as the result of care or pains
   a. Ushers took an **accurate** count of the people assembled* in the theatre.
   b. Emma's vision* was so **accurate** that she didn't need glasses.
   c. In writing on the topic,* Vergil used **accurate** information.

9. **microscope** (mī' krə skōp) instrument with a lens for making objects larger so that one can see things more clearly
   a. The students used a **microscope** to see the miniature* insect.
   b. Young Jonas Salk wanted to get a glimpse* of things he couldn't see with just his eyes, so his father bought him a **microscope.**
   c. Using a **microscope,** the scientist was able to probe* into the habits of germs.

10. **grateful** (grāt' fəl) feeling gratitude; thankful
    a. The majority* of pupils felt **grateful** for Mr. Ash's help.
    b. We were **grateful** that the gloomy* weather cleared up on Saturday.
    c. In his letter, Waldo told how **grateful** he was for the loan.

11. **cautious** (kô′ shəs) very careful; never taking chances
    a. Be **cautious** when you choose your opponent.*
    b. Good authors are **cautious** not to exaggerate* when they write.
    c. If the rain is falling in torrents,* it is best to drive **cautiously.**

12. **confident** (kän′ fə dənt) firmly believing; certain; sure
    a. Judge Emery was **confident** he could solve the conflict.*
    b. When he lifted the burden,* Scotty was **confident** he could carry it.
    c. Annette was **confident** she would do well as a nurse.

---

**Which of the words studied in this lesson is suggested by the picture?**

---

*Read the following story to see how the new words are used in it.*

**A Valuable New Discovery**

The laser is a marvelous new device that sends out a **slender,** concentrated beam of light, a light that **surpasses** the light at the sun's surface. So **vast** is the laser beam's power that it has without a **doubt** the **capacity** to vaporize* any substance located anywhere on earth. The laser can **penetrate** steel, **pierce** a diamond, or make an **accurate** die for wire so thin that it can be seen only with a **microscope.**

**Grateful** eye surgeons report that they have used laser beams to repair the retinas in some fortunate* patients by creating tiny scars that joined the retina to the eyeball. Pioneering* medical men are making **cautious** exploration* into cancer cures with the laser, **confident** that they will alter* the course of this brutal* disease.

**Place one of the new words in each of the blanks below.**

1. Little Paul was _____ that he got the Christmas present he asked for.
2. I _____ that you can break Mark Spitz's world swimming record.
3. My mother used to say that I was as _____ as a toothpick.
4. Be _____ about swimming right after eating a meal.
5. The map he drew of our neighborhood was not very _____.
6. In Superman comics, the only thing Superman couldn't _____ was lead.
7. When my family went to look for a new house, we had a _____ choice.
8. Modern highways far _____ the old dirt roads of yesterday.
9. The jar was filled to _____.
10. We were all very _____ that Duane would pass his exams.
11. The _____ used by my biology teacher is very expensive.
12. The music was so loud that I thought that it would _____ my eardrums.

---

**Synonyms.** Circle the word that most nearly expresses the meaning of the word printed in heavy black type.

1. **penetrate** the skin
   a. pass through
   b. moisten
   c. burn
   d. protect

2. electron **microscope**
   a. rangefinder
   b. reflection mirror
   c. optical enlargening instrument
   d. three-dimensional focuser

3. **confident** speaker
   a. certain
   b. aboveboard
   c. reasonable
   d. well-informed

4. **slender** forms
   a. round and curvy
   b. bright and shiny
   c. colorful and attractive
   d. long and thin

5. **accurate** information
   a. error-free
   b. endless
   c. available
   d. remarkable

6. taste that cannot be **surpassed**
   a. pursued*
   b. excelled*
   c. seen
   d. approved

7. an unlimited **capacity**
   a. ability to store
   b. attention to detail
   c. resistance* to change
   d. talent

8. move **cautiously**
   a. very carefully
   b. with exaggeration
   c. hurriedly
   d. in a satisfying manner

9. **grateful** for the help given
   a. tearful
   b. proud
   c. thankful
   d. persuaded*

10. **vast** wilderness
    a. unknown
    b. enormous
    c. untamed
    d. quiet

11. a road that **pierces** the dense* jungle
    a. cuts through
    b. winds in and out of
    c. runs parallel to
    d. avoids

12. innocent beyond a shadow of a **doubt**
    a. lack of certainty
    b. lack of freedom
    c. lack of vision*
    d. lack of courage

---

**Spotlight on:**    **confident**—Have you ever wondered why the name Fido is often given to a dog? The root of the word *confident* tells you. *Fidere* meant "trust" in Latin and the dog, man's best friend, has been traditionally considered trusty and faithful to his master. However, too much trust can bring trouble: look up the meaning of *confidence man*.

# Lesson 17

"Word by word the book is made."

French proverb

**Words To Learn This Week**

appeal
addict
wary
aware
misfortune
avoid
wretched
keg
nourish
harsh
quantity
opt

1. **appeal** (ə pēl′) attraction; interest; to urge
   a. Anything Jorge could get at wholesale* price had a great **appeal** for him.
   b. My boss always **appeals** to his employees* to work swiftly and neatly.
   c. I found her clothing designs to be enormously* **appealing.**

2. **addict** (ad′ ikt) one who cannot break away from a habit or practice; **addicted** unable to break a habit
   a. Because he was a heroin **addict,** it was essential* for Carlos to get the drug each day.
   b. Marcia became flabby* because she was **addicted** to ice cream sodas.
   c. Those who take aspirins and other pain-killers regularly should realize that they may become drug **addicts,** too.

3. **wary** (wãr′ ē) on one's guard against danger or trickery; cautious*
   a. Marilyn's mother told her to be **wary** of strangers with a gleam* in their eye.
   b. After Orlando had been the victim of a cheat, he was **wary** of those who said they wanted to help him.
   c. Living in a polluted* city makes you **wary** of the air you breathe.

4. **aware** (ə wãr′) knowing; realizing
   a. Donna was **aware** of her tendency* to exaggerate.*
   b. It was some time before the police became **aware** of the brawl* which was taking place on the street.
   c. The only way to gain knowledge* is to be **aware** of everything around you.

5. **misfortune** (mis fôr′ chən) bad luck
   a. It was my **misfortune** that our car wasn't thoroughly* checked before the trip through the desert.
   b. Being bitten by the vicious* dog was quite a **misfortune** for Tommy.
   c. I had the **misfortune** of working for a greedy* man.

6. **avoid** (ə void′) keep away from; keep out of the way of
   a. If you are fortunate* you can **avoid** people who are trying to deceive* you.
   b. There was no way to **avoid** noticing her beautiful green eyes.
   c. **Avoid** getting into a brawl* if you can.

7. **wretched** (retch′ id) very unsatisfactory; miserable
   a. I feel **wretched** after a night when I've scarcely* slept.
   b. There was unanimous* agreement that we had seen a **wretched** movie.
   c. Toby had **wretched** luck at the gambling tables.

8. **keg** (keg) small barrel, usually holding less than ten gallons
   a. The corner saloon uses numerous* **kegs** of beer on a Saturday night.
   b. "Get a **keg** of nails," the carpenter shouted at me.
   c. It is obvious* to me that the situation is filled with peril,* a real powder **keg** if I ever saw one.

9. **nourish** (nėr′ ish) make or keep alive and well, with food; feed; develop an attitude
   a. A diet of **nourishing** food is served to every hospital patient.
   b. It was easy to detect* that the skinny boy was not well **nourished.**
   c. After the operation, our doctor plans to **nourish** my mother with vitamins and good food.

10. **harsh** (härsh) rough to the touch, taste, eye, or ear; sharp
    a. The law is **harsh** on people who go around menacing* others.
    b. Looking at his cigarette, Phil realized it was absurd* to inhale such **harsh** smoke.
    c. Hazel altered* her tone of voice from a **harsh** one to a soft tone.

11. **quantity** (kwän′ tə tē) amount
    a. I never neglect* to carry a small **quantity** of money with me.
    b. Who believes that **quantity** is better than quality?
    c. A large **quantity** of meat is always stored in our freezer.

12. **opt** (opt) choose or favor; select
    a. If you give me an ice cream choice, I'll **opt** for chocolate.
    b. Our cheerleaders plan to **opt** for new sweaters.
    c. On Friday, three of my buddies will **opt** to go into the navy.

---

*Read the following story to see how the new words are used in it.*

### A Cup of Coffee?

The drink with the most **appeal** for Americans is still coffee, but coffee **addicts** had better be **wary** of the instant forms. Greedy for customers and confident* they won't lose them, companies will put their product in any instant form—liquid, powder, chips—and the coffee drinker, **aware** of his **misfortune,** finds it hard to **avoid** some of the more **wretched** instant products. The **harsh** fact is that an enormous* **quantity** of instant coffee is being sold, no doubt,* to **nourish** the popular demand for convenience. A **keg** of real coffee may become a museum piece as more and more people **opt** for instant coffee.

---

**Which of the words studied in this lesson is suggested by the picture?**

**Place one of the new words in each of the blanks below.**

1. Sometimes it is best to _____ being too nice to strangers.
2. I wasn't _____ that there were concerts in the park on Tuesdays.
3. We bought a large _____ of potato chips for the party.
4. Rock 'n roll music just doesn't _____ to me.
5. My aunt was in _____ health and had to have nurses on twenty-four hour duty.
6. The _____ smoke from the fireplace burned my eyes.
7. It was quite a _____ that Beverly's husband died in an automobile accident.
8. If I had to _____ for a new career, it would be medicine.
9. It is smart to be _____ of foods whose contents are not listed on the package.
10. The judge denounced* the thief for stealing a _____ of molasses.
11. A candy bar will not _____ you the way a piece of meat will.
12. Baxter took pep pills regularly and became a drug _____ without realizing it.

---

**Matching.** Match the 12 new words in Column I with the definitions in Column II.

Column I

_____ 1. opt
_____ 2. quantity
_____ 3. misfortune
_____ 4. nourish
_____ 5. appeal
_____ 6. harsh
_____ 7. addict
_____ 8. keg
_____ 9. wretched
_____ 10. wary
_____ 11. avoid
_____ 12. aware

Column II

a. attraction
b. miserable
c. one who cannot break a habit
d. realizing
e. small barrel
f. cautious
g. keep away from
h. rough to the touch, taste, eye, or ear
i. amount
j. choose or favor
k. bad luck
l. make or keep alive and well with food

---

**Spotlight on:**    **keg**—The history of a word tells us something of the habits and traditions of a people. What, for example, can you deduce about the trade and customs of early Englishmen from the fact that the word *keg* came into our language from the Icelandic word *kaggi?* Perhaps the hardy people of that northern land found good use for what they could store in those containers.

---

# Lesson 18

"Without knowing the force of words, it is impossible to know men."

Confucius, *Analects*

Words To Learn
This Week

tragedy
pedestrian
glance
budget
nimble
manipulate
reckless
horrid
rave
economical
lubricate
ingenious

1. **tragedy** (traj′ə dē) a very sad or terrible happening; a sad play
   a. It was a **tragedy** that some pioneers* were killed on their way west.
   b. If you had your choice between seeing a comedy or a **tragedy,** which play would you choose?
   c. Harry's enormous* jealousy* led to the **tragedy** in their family.

2. **pedestrian** (pə des′ tri ən) person who goes on foot; walker
   a. After driving a bus all day, Norris liked to be a **pedestrian** and take long, casual* walks in the evening.
   b. The police say it is urgent* that **pedestrians** stay on the sidewalk.
   c. I don't doubt* that a **pedestrian** can get places faster than a car in downtown traffic.

3. **glance** (glans) to look at quickly; a quick look
   a. The observant* driver **glanced** at the accident at the side of the road.
   b. I took one **glance** at the wretched* animal and turned away.
   c. Thompson identified* the burglar after a **glance** at the photograph in the police station.

4. **budget** (buj′ it) estimate of the amount of money that can be spent for different purposes in a given time
   a. We had to decrease* the **budget** this year because our club is broke.
   b. The prominent* executive presented her **budget** to the Board of Directors.
   c. When my mother draws up her **budget** for the week, she sets aside a goodly sum for nourishing* food.

5. **nimble** (nim′ bəl) active and sure-footed; quick moving; light and quick
   a. Although Dusty was a miniature* poodle, he was **nimble** enough to fight bigger dogs.
   b. The **nimble** policeman leaped over the fence to pursue* the car thief.
   c. At his press conference, the Commissioner was quite **nimble** in avoiding* the difficult questions.

6. **manipulate** (mə nip′ yə lāt) handle or treat skillfully
   a. Scientists must know how to **manipulate** their microscopes.*
   b. While Mr. Baird **manipulated** the puppets, Fran spoke to the audience.
   c. The wounded pilot **manipulated** the radio dial until he made contact.

7. **reckless** (rek′ lis) careless; heedless; wild
   a. We must not ignore* **reckless** drivers; we must take them off the road.
   b. After breaking his hand fighting **recklessly,** Arthur decided to be more cautious* in the future.
   c. The **reckless** smoker ignited* the entire forest.

8. **horrid** (hôr′ id) terrible; frightful
   a. Janey avoided* staring at the **horrid** man's face.
   b. It is simply **horrid** the way cars pollute* the air we breathe.
   c. When Mary was good, she was very good, but when she was bad, she was **horrid.**

9. **rave** (rāv) talk wildly
   a. Shortly after taking the drug, the addict* began to **rave** and foam at the mouth.
   b. Speedy **raved** that his car had the capacity* to reach 120 miles per hour.
   c. Sadie was confident* that Mr. Stebbe would **rave** about her essay.

10. **economical** (ē kə näm′ i kl) not wasting money or time
    a. I find it **economical** to shop in the large supermarkets.
    b. Marissa was praised for her **economical** management of the budget.*
    c. The President made Congress aware* of the need to be more **economical.**

11. **lubricate** (lōō brə kāt) make (machinery) smooth and easy to work by putting on oil, grease, or a similar substance
    a. The bulky* wheels of a railroad train must be **lubricated** each week.
    b. A large quantity* of grease is needed to **lubricate** an airplane engine.
    c. When a watch is **lubricated,** it keeps more accurate* time.

12. **ingenious** (in jēn′ yəs) having great mental ability; clever
    a. Bernie devised* an **ingenious** plan to cheat on his income tax.
    b. Rube Goldberg was a journalist* who won fame for his **ingenious** inventions.
    c. The master spy had an **ingenious** way of passing secrets to the agent.

---

*Read the following story to see how the new words are used in it.*

### The Challenge* of the Small Car

The auto makers in Detroit barely survived* the **tragedy** of 1956. That was the year the consumer became aware* of the Volkswagen, and the auto market was forever altered.* Once Americans got a **glance** at this low-priced, **nimble,** small car that one could **manipulate** so easily, they frequently* refused those **horrid** Detroit monsters with eight cylinders and ten miles to each gallon of gasoline. Many **pedestrians,** previously uninterested in owning a car, began to purchase small foreign cars.

Conservative, as well as **reckless** drivers, found the price within their **budget** and became customers.

Volkswagen owners would **rave** about their **economical** cars, telling everyone how little gas they used and how infrequently* they needed to be **lubricated.** Volkswagen still is one of the most popular* small cars sold in America, even though it has fallen behind the autos of the **ingenious** Japanese manufacturers.

---

### Place one of the new words in each of the blanks below.

1. Try not to be _____ when you drive a car, especially at night.
2. The brilliant investigator found an _____ answer to the problem.
3. I find it more _____ to buy a monthly train ticket than to pay for each ride each day.
4. If you continue to _____ about the play, everyone will think you are a relative of the author.
5. I took one _____ and I knew it was Frank Sinatra.
6. Every week Mrs. Evans made a _____ covering the essential* sums she would have to spend.
7. The coach knew how to _____ the players to do what he wanted.
8. Bobby's job at the gas station was to _____ all the cars after they had been worked on.
9. When someone you love dies, it is a _____.
10. Journalists* reported that the dropping of the bombs was a _____ act.
11. The car leaped up on the sidewalk, struck a _____, and then crashed into the bakery's window.
12. Whirling* across the stage, the _____ ballet dancer captured our hearts.

---

### Exercise

*Now make up your own sentences, one for each of the new words you have just been taught.*

1. _____
2. _____
3. _____

4. _____

5. _____

6. _____

7. _____

8. _____

9. _____

10. _____

11. _____

12. _____

**Spotlight on:**    **pedestrian**—You have learned the use of this word as a noun, but the word undergoes an interesting change when it is used as an adjective. A *pedestrian speech*, for example, is very dull and commonplace. It moves along very slowly. Can you see how this meaning is related to "going on foot"? Another uncomplimentary use of the same root is *pedant*. Find the meaning.

**Which of the words studied in this lesson is suggested by the picture?**

# Word Review #3

These exercises are based on some of the words which were included in Lessons 13–18.

**A.** In each of the parentheses below you will find two choices. Pick the one that fits better.
1. It broke our hearts to see the suffering caused by the (famine, wretched) in Africa.
2. Watching the piano player's (nimble, wary) fingers was great entertainment.
3. The once-rich manufacturer was trying hard to (revive, surpass) interest in his product.
4. Lois receive a pat on the back for her (unruly, mature) behavior.
5. Only if you (alter, avoid) the plans for the vacation will I be able to go along with you.
6. Bruce's (reckless, cautious) way of driving caused many accidents.
7. Since you are unwilling to (pursue, duplicate) the matter, I think we ought to forget about it.
8. Parker's (casual, economical) way of handling his money saved a fortune for his family.
9. Every member of our club agreed to the new rule and it was passed (unanimously, confidently).
10. Our cellar is filled to (capacity, quantity) with old furniture and other junk.

**B. Opposites.** In Column I are ten words from Lessons 13–18. Match them correctly with their *opposite* meanings in Column II.

| Column I | Column II |
|---|---|
| 1. ingenious | a. starve |
| 2. nourish | b. make smaller |
| 3. commence | c. stupid |
| 4. hazy | d. thick |
| 5. slender | e. good luck |
| 6. expand | f. clear |
| 7. misfortune | g. driver |
| 8. harsh | h. stay at home |
| 9. migrate | i. smooth |
| 10. pedestrian | j. finish |

**C.** Which of the vocabulary choices in parentheses fits best in these newspaper headlines?
1. **"Send Food To Relieve _____ In Africa**     (Famine, Underdog, Reckless, Economical)
2. **City Council In _____ Vote To Lower Taxes**     (Casual, Fortunate, Unanimous, Ingenious)
3. **Henry Ford Honored As _____ In Auto Industry**     (Sacred, Pioneer, Rival, Brutal)
4. **Millions _____ To Warmth Of The Southwest**     (Appeal, Surpass, Expand, Migrate)
5. **Producer To _____ Musical Comedy Hit Of The 1920's**     (Appeal, Commence, Revive, Pledge)
6. **"Be _____ Of Get-Rich-Quick Schemes," Warns Banker**     (Wary, Reckless, Grateful, Confident)
7. **Referees Fail To Control _____ Hockey Game**     (Nimble, Duplicate, Unruly, Vast)
8. **Dieter Praised For _____ Figure**     (Observant, Slender, Bewildered, Casual)
9. **Training Film Shows How To Avoid Being _____ Driver**     (Nimble, Wary, Reckless, Accurate)
10. **_____ Dog Bites Three Children**     (Vicious, Wary, Harsh, Sacred)

**D.** From the list of words below choose the word that means:
1. self-assurance and boldness *but* in the phrase "_____ man" is not complimentary
2. the first in a new field *and* began as the French word for "foot soldier"
3. a competitor *but originally* meant one who lives across the river
4. a ship *as well as* a hollow utensil such as a pot, kettle, or dish
5. push *as well as* pierce or lunge
6. correct *as well as* update
7. volume or ability to learn *and* occurs in the phrases "full to _____" and "operate at _____"
8. give food *as well as* develop an attitude or habit
9. a type of drama *as well as* a sad event
10. talk wildly *but also* a form of praise

| | | | | | |
|---|---|---|---|---|---|
| manipulate | quantity | thrust | penetrate | rival | bewildered |
| rave | pioneer | duplicate | capacity | pledge | observant |
| appeal | casual | whirling | tragedy | gleam | identify |
| wary | unruly | confidence | expand | nourish | persist |
| wretched | brawl | surpass | sacred | vessel | revise |

# Lesson 19

"For one word a man is often deemed to be wise, and for one word he is often deemed to be foolish. We should be careful indeed what we say.

Confucius, *Analects*

1. **harvest** (här′ vist) gathering in of grain or other food crops
   a. This year's **harvest** was adequate* to feed all our people.
   b. The farmer decided to expand* his fields so that he would get a bigger **harvest.**
   c. If the **harvest** is poor, there is always the possibility of a famine.*

2. **abundant** (ə bun′ dənt) more than enough; very plentiful
   a. It is urgent* that the hospital have an **abundant** supply of blood.
   b. An **abundant** harvest* was predicted* by the Secretary of Agriculture.
   c. In recent* years an **abundant** number of complaints have disturbed the telephone company.

3. **uneasy** (un ēz′ ē) restless; disturbed; anxious
   a. Mrs. Spinner was **uneasy** about letting her son play in the vicinity* of the railroad tracks.
   b. The treasurer was **uneasy** about the company's budget.*
   c. Arnold felt **uneasy** about the meeting even though he tried to act in a casual* manner.

4. **calculate** (kal′ kyəlāt) find out by adding, subtracting, multiplying, or dividing; figure
   a. The cook had to **calculate** the number of diners to see whether he could decrease* his order for meat.
   b. In order to see how expensive* the car was, the buyer **calculated** the tax and other charges.
   c. I used an abacus to **calculate** my average.

5. **absorb** (ab sôrb′) take in or suck up (liquids); interest greatly.
   a. The sponge **absorbed** the beer which had leaked from the keg.*
   b. Our bodies must **absorb** those things which will nourish* them.
   c. I became **absorbed** in what the teacher was saying and did not hear the bell ring.

6. **estimate** (es′ tə māt) form a judgment or opinion about; guess
   a. A.J. Foyt **estimated** that the auto race would commence* at nine o'clock.
   b. I try to avoid* making **estimates** on things I know nothing about.
   c. In your **estimate,** who will be victorious* in this conflict?*

7. **morsel** (môr′ səl) a small bite; mouthful; tiny amount
   a. When Reynaldo went into the restaurant, he pledged* to eat every **morsel** on his plate.
   b. Suzanne was reluctant* to try even a **morsel** of the lobster.
   c. If you had a **morsel** of intelligence, you would be uneasy,* too.

8. **quota** (kwō′ tə) share of a total due from or to a particular state, district, person, etc.
   a. The company revealed* a **quota** of jobs reserved for college students.
   b. There was a **quota** placed on the number of people who could migrate* here from China.
   c. Lieutenant Dugan doubted* that a **quota** had been placed on the number of parking tickets each policeofficer was supposed to give out.

9. **threat** (thret) sign or cause of possible evil or harm
   a. There is always the horrid* **threat** that my job will be abolished.*
   b. It is absurd* to think that a tiny bug could be a **threat** to a person.
   c. You can be arrested for making a **threat** against someone's life.

10. **ban** (ban) prohibit; forbid
    a. The group unanimously* voted to **ban** all people who were under six feet.
    b. Health officials are trying to expand* their field in order to **ban** cigarette advertising from newspapers and magazines.
    c. I want to **ban** all outsiders from our discussion on security.*

11. **panic** (pan' ik) unreasoning fear; fear spreading through a group of people so that they lose control of themselves
    a. The leader of the lost group appealed* to them not to **panic.**
    b. When the danger was exaggerated,* a few people started to **panic.**
    c. The source* of **panic** in the crowd was a man with a gun.

12. **appropriate** (ə prō′ prē it) fit; set apart for some special use
    a. At an **appropriate** time, the chief promised to reveal* his plan.
    b. The lawn was an **appropriate** setting for Eileen's wedding.
    c. After some **appropriate** prayers, the dinner was served.

---

*Read the following story to see how the new words are used in it.*

### Protecting Our Health

Pick an apple, a tomato, a peach — no worms in the **harvest.** We are familiar with the **abundant** use of pesticides by farmers, but today's chemists are becoming **uneasy.** They **calculate** that there are 45,000 different pesticides, and all of them can be **absorbed** by the fruit on which they are sprayed. The chemists **estimate** that every **morsel** we eat in the future may contain a deadly **quota** of pesticide. The tragedy* will come slowly but the **threat** is real. These government chemists do not suggest that we **ban** pesticides. They are cautious* and do not easily **panic.** What is needed, they say, are **appropriate,** budgeted* doses that will not pollute* our food.

---

**Which of the words studied in this lesson is suggested by the picture?**

**Place one of the new words in each of the blanks below.**

1. The committee recommended that we _____ all dangerous foods.
2. Dave had his _____ of cookies for the day.
3. You should always make sure that you have an _____ supply of gasoline for a long trip.
4. The rain was _____ into the concrete when it was dry.
5. Is this inexpensive* dress_____for a formal wedding?
6. How much do you _____ that horse is worth?
7. Helen Hayes had an _____ feeling as she went on to the stage for the first time.
8. When you are in trouble the worst thing to do is to _____.
9. The farmers had a good _____ of corn this year.
10. We _____ all the figures and came to one solid answer.
11. Every_____the cook prepared was tasty.
12. The _____ of snow caused us to change our holiday plans.

---

**Choose the Correct Word.** Circle the word in parentheses that best fits the sense of the sentence.

1. When the food supply is (abundant, appropriate), there is no reason for anyone to go hungry.
2. Some people believe that the (threat, quota) of nuclear war is a very real danger of the twentieth century.
3. If you feel (uneasy, appropriate) about being capable of doing this work, please let me help you get started.
4. It is important not to (panic, calculate) in emergency situations.
5. Farmers hope their labors will be rewarded with a plentiful (harvest, morsel).
6. To (calculate, absorb) whether I need an A or a B on my math final, I had to first figure my average to date.
7. It's difficult to believe that even today there are school boards that (ban, harvest) books such as *The Catcher in the Rye*.
8. The dish looked so strange and smelled so foul, that I found it difficult to taste a (morsel, quota) of the meal our host had prepared.
9. I can't possibly (absorb, ban) such an enormous* amount of information in just two hours.
10. Many countries have strict (quotas, threats) on the number of immigrants they admit each year.
11. If my (estimate, quota) is correct, the homes presently under construction will mean about 200 new elementary school students in the district next year.
12. The (appropriate, abundant) behavior for different situations is something we all learn as part of growing up.

---

**Spotlight on:**   **calculate**—A Roman "taxi" driver used to charge his customers by figuring out, or calculating, the number of pebbles (Latin word—*calculus*) that dropped into a basket in a given time.

---

# Lesson 20

*"Words are, of course, the most powerful drug used by mankind."*

Rudyard Kipling, *Speech*

## Words To Learn This Week

emerge
jagged
linger
ambush
crafty
defiant
vigor
perish
fragile
captive
prosper
devour

1. **emerge** (i mėrj′) come out; come up; come into view
   a. When the fight was over, the underdog* **emerged** the winner.
   b. You have to be nimble* to **emerge** from the narrow opening in five seconds.
   c. What **emerged** from the bottle was a blend* of fruit juices.

2. **jagged** (jag′ id) with sharp points sticking out; unevenly cut or torn
   a. Being reckless,* Rudy didn't watch out for the **jagged** steel.
   b. It's an enormous* job to smooth the **jagged** edge of a fence.
   c. Leslie's hair was so **jagged** it was scarcely* possible to tell that it had just been cut.

3. **linger** (ling′ gər) stay on; go slowly as if unwilling to leave
   a. The odor didn't vanish* but **lingered** on for weeks.
   b. Some traditions* **linger** on long after they have lost their meanings.
   c. After the campus* closed for the summer, some students **lingered** on, reluctant* to go home.

4. **ambush** (am′ bush) a trap in which soldiers or other enemies hide to make a surprise attack
   a. The **ambush** became a tragedy* for those who attempted it because they were all killed.
   b. General Taylor raved* about the ingenious* **ambush** he planned.
   c. The troops lay in **ambush** in the dense* woods all through the night.

5. **crafty** (kraf′ tē) skillful in deceiving others; sly; tricky
   a. His **crafty** mind prepared a comprehensive* plan to defraud* his partners.
   b. Leo didn't use brutal* strength against his opponents,* but he used his **crafty** bag of tricks to beat them.
   c. The Indians did not fall for the **crafty** ambush.*

6. **defiant** (di fī′ ənt) openly resisting; challenging*
   a. "I refuse to be manipulated,"* the **defiant** young woman told her father.
   b. Professor Carlyle was **defiant** of any attempt to disprove his theory.*
   c. **Defiant** of everyone, the addict* refused to be helped.

7. **vigor** (vig′ ər) active strength or force
   a. Having a great deal of **vigor,** Jason was able to excel* in all sports.
   b. Tom Thumb made up for size by having more **vigor** than most people.
   c. Putting all her **vigor** into the argument, Patsy persuaded* me to let her drive.

8. **perish** (per′ ish) be destroyed; die
   a. Unless the plant gets water for its roots to absorb,* it will **perish.**
   b. Custer and all his men **perished** at the Little Big Horn.
   c. We are trying to make sure that democracy will never **perish** from this earth.

9. **fragile** (fraj′ əl) easily broken, damaged, or destroyed; delicate
   a. The expensive* glassware is very **fragile.**
   b. Things made out of plywood have a tendency* to be **fragile.**
   c. On the box was a label which read, "**Fragile!** Handle with care!"

10. **captive** (kap′ tiv) prisoner
    a. The major was grateful* to be released after having been held **captive** for two years.
    b. Until the sheriff got them out, the two boys were held **captive** in the barn.
    c. Placido Domingo can hold an audience **captive** with his marvelous singing voice.

11. **prosper** (pros′ pər) be successful; have good fortune
    a. Howard Hughes owned numerous* businesses and most of them **prospered.**
    b. No one should **prosper** from the misfortunes* of his or her friends.
    c. The annual* report showed that the new business was **prospering.**
12. **devour** (di vour′) eat hungrily; absorb* completely; take in greedily*
    a. It was a horrid* sight to see the lion **devour** the lamb.
    b. The animal doctor was pleased to see the terrier **devour** the dog food.
    c. My aunt **devours** four or five mystery books each week.

---

*Read the following story to see how the new words are used in it.*

### A Home Where the Buffalo Roam

Even today in South Dakota a cowboy **emerges** from behind a **jagged** rock where he has **lingered** in **ambush** waiting for the **crafty** buffalo to appear. Although not wild—they are raised on vast* ranches—the gallant,* **defiant** bison need to be hunted with the same **vigor** cowboys showed a century* ago. For a while, Americans thought the buffalo would **perish** from the earth; fortunately* the buffalo is far from being such a **fragile** animal. Now more or less **captive,** the buffalo, an estimated* 10,000, are raised for profit by ranchers who **prosper** from the sale of buffalo meat. When did you **devour** your last morsel* of tasty buffalo meat?

---

**Which of the words studied in this lesson is suggested by the picture?**

**Place one of the new words in each of the blanks below.**

1.  If we do not do something about pollution,* we may _____ from this earth.
2.  The _____ edge of that sheet of metal is very dangerous.
3.  We were held _____ by the sinister* enemy for ten days.
4.  The bank teller's _____ plan to steal a million dollars didn't succeed.
5.  I like to _____ on until everyone else has left the theatre.
6.  My parents taught me not to be _____ of authority.
7.  Did the _____ of the Lebanese soldiers fail?
8.  Business persons can _____ if they are honest with their customers.
9.  A new star has just _____ from the rock music world.
10. I can _____ a steak in two minutes when I am hungry.
11. With a surprising show of _____, the old woman swam up and down the pool six times!
12. A lack* of calcium in Tyrone's diet caused his bones to be quite _____.

---

**Antonyms (opposites).** Circle the word that most nearly expresses the opposite meaning of the word printed in heavy black type.

1.  **emerge**
    a.  go back
    b.  involve
    c.  disturb
    d.  ruin
    e.  amuse

2.  **captive**
    a.  reluctant*
    b.  free to leave
    c.  active
    d.  rapidly constructed
    e.  solitary*

3.  **ambush**
    a.  openly attack
    b.  readily remove
    c.  secretly strive
    d.  quickly determine
    e.  water thoroughly

4.  **fragile**
    a.  demanding
    b.  strudy
    c.  careful
    d.  genuine
    e.  shrewd

5.  **devour**
    a.  charge
    b.  figure out
    c.  nourish*
    d.  leave untouched
    e.  perist*

6.  **jagged**
    a.  confusing
    b.  smooth-edged
    c.  linked together
    d.  microscopic*
    e.  unspoiled

7.  **defiant**
    a.  ready to act
    b.  willing to obey
    c.  reliable
    d.  vulgar
    e.  evasive

8.  **linger**
    a.  underestimate*
    b.  exclude
    c.  wither
    d.  leave quickly
    e.  neglect*

9.  **vigor**
    a.  lack of strength
    b.  lack of funds
    c.  lack of ability
    d.  lack of understanding
    e.  lack of tradition*

10. **crafty**
    a.  honest
    b.  wretched
    c.  vulgar
    d.  mystical
    e.  absurd*

11. **prosper**
    a.  be unsuccessful
    b.  manipulate*
    c.  penetrate*
    d.  assemble*
    e.  license

12. **perish**
    a.  fight
    b.  live
    c.  ban*
    d.  resent*
    e.  molest*

**Spotlight on:**  **ambush**—What kind of hiding place would best protect a person who wanted to ambush an enemy? The clue is in the word itself. Of course, the bushes or woods provided the greatest safety for the attacker. The bushes are better hidden in the word *ambuscade*, but the meaning is the same. Now you have gained two words in one stroke.

---

# Lesson 21

"In a multitude of words there will certainly be error."

Chinese proverb

**Words To Learn
This Week**

plea
weary
collide
confirm
verify
anticipate
dilemma
detour
merit
transmit
relieve
baffle

1. **plea** (plē) request; appeal; that which is asked of another
   a. The employees* turned in a **plea** to their boss for higher pay.
   b. The President's **plea** to release the captives* was denied by the enemy.
   c. In court today, the judge consented* to the lawyer's **plea** for a light sentence.

2. **weary** (wēr' ē) tired
   a. I am **weary** of debating* the same topic* all day.
   b. The farmer grew **weary** of bringing in the harvest* every year for the past forty summers.
   c. Let me rest my **weary** bones here before the march commences.*

3. **collide** (kə līd') come together with force
   a. When the two autos **collided,** the people in the fragile* smaller car perished.*
   b. Committees are exploring* ways of keeping cars from **colliding.**
   c. In my estimate* the two bicycles **collided** at five o'clock.

4. **confirm** (kən fėrm') prove to be true or correct; make certain
   a. The way Victor talked back to his mother **confirmed** that he was defiant.*
   b. A probe* of the criminal's background **confirmed** that he had been in jail numerous* times.
   c. Years of research **confirmed** the theory* that smoking is harmful.

5. **verify** (ver' ə fī) prove to be true; confirm*
   a. A "yes man" is an employee* who will **verify** everything the boss says.
   b. I was there as a witness to **verify** the charges against the bus driver.
   c. The data* I turned in were **verified** by the clerks in our office.

6. **anticipate** (an tis' ə pāt) look forward to; expect
   a. We **anticipate** a panic* if the news is revealed* to the public.
   b. Harriet **anticipated** the approach* of the mailman with fright.
   c. With his weird* powers, Lonnie was able to **anticipate** the ringing of the telephone.

7. **dilemma** (də lem' ə) situation requiring a choice between two evils; a difficult choice
   a. It is sensible not to panic* in the face of a **dilemma.**
   b. Lottie faced the **dilemma** of whether to approve of the operation or not.
   c. In "The Lady or the Tiger," the hero had the **dilemma** of which door to open.

8. **detour** (dē' toor) a roundabout way
   a. Pop was uneasy* about taking the **detour** in this strange town.
   b. In order to evade* city traffic, Anthony took a **detour.**
   c. The **detour** took us ten miles off our course.

9. **merit** (mer' it) goodness; worth; value
   a. There is little **merit** in lying to those you love.
   b. My brother was promoted because of **merit,** not because of friendship.
   c. Do you think the tradition* of marriage has any **merit?**

10. **transmit** (trans mit') send over; pass on; pass along; let through
    a. Garcia's message was **transmitted** to the appropriate* people.
    b. Scientists can now **transmit** messages from space vessels* to earth.
    c. Our local radio station does not **transmit** broadcasts after midnight.

11. **relieve** (ri lēv′) make less; make easier; reduce the pain of; replace; release; free
   a. The pills **relieved** the pain from the wound I received in the conflict.*
   b. A majority* of the population* wanted to **relieve** the mayor of his duty.
   c. The peace agreement **relieved** us of the threat* of an attack.
12. **baffle** (baf′əl) be too hard to understand or solve
   a. How so mediocre* a player earned so much money **baffled** me.
   b. The topic* of relativity is a **baffling** one.
   c. Sherlock Holmes would undoubtedly* have been **baffled** by the way the crime was committed.

---

*Read the following story to see how the new words are used in it.*

### Safety in the Air

The most persistent* **plea** of **weary** pilots has always been for a machine that would warn them that they were about to **collide** with an oncoming airplane. Records **confirm** that the number of collisions is increasing each year, and pilots **verify** hundreds of reports of near misses. Recently a system that would electronically **anticipate** oncoming airplanes was devised,* and the pilot's **dilemma** to dive or to climb, to **detour** to left or right, may be solved. The system has **merit,** though, only if every plane is equipped to **transmit** and receive a signal to and from an oncoming plane. But most aviation experts feel that only a system that watches every airplane in the sky will **relieve** a problem that tends to **baffle** every one who attempts to find a solution.

---

**Which of the words studied in this lesson is suggested by the picture?**

**Place one of the new words in each of the blanks below.**

1. The first time a message was _____ over a telegraph was in 1840.
2. Can you _____ that this is your handwriting?
3. I took a _____ to avoid traffic.
4. We were all very _____ after the long trip.
5. There is _____ in being a good listener.
6. The judge listened to the burglar's _____ of not guilty.
7. The runner and catcher were about to _____ at home plate.
8. Tyrone was _____ that he didn't have any more work to do.
9. When you run a company you have at least one new _____ every day to solve.
10. Did you _____ our reservations at the hotel?
11. We were_____as to who murdered the wretched* old man.
12. After having been married to Arthur for thirty years, Selma could _____ everything he was going to say.

(NOTE: You might have used the same word in Sentences 2 and 10.)

---

**Which Word Means.** From the list of 12 new words that follows, choose the one that corresponds to each definition below.

| plea | weary | collide | confirm |
|------|-------|---------|---------|
| verify | anticipate | dilemma | detour |
| merit | transmit | relieve | baffle |

1. a roundabout way _____
2. that which is asked of another _____
3. come together with force _____
4. pass along _____
5. be too hard to understand _____
6. goodness; worth; value _____
7. make easier; replace _____
8. tired _____
9. make certain _____
10. a difficult choice _____
11. prove to be true _____
12. expect _____

(NOTE: The same words could be used for definitions 9 and 11.)

---

**Spotlight on:**    **dilemma**—The sport of bull fighting provides us with a vivid expression—being on the horns of a dilemma—to describe a situation in which we are faced with two choices, each equally unpleasant. It is as if we were asked to choose which horn of a bull we prefer to be gored by.

---

# Lesson 22

"Words are like leaves, and where they most abound
Much fruit of sense beneath is rarely found."

Alexander Pope, *Essay on Criticism*

1. **warden** (wôr′ dən) keeper; guard; person in charge of a prison
   a. The **warden** found himself facing two hundred defiant* prisoners.
   b. A cautious* **warden** always has to anticipate* the possibility of an escape.
   c. When the journalists* asked to meet with **Warden** Thomas, he sent word that he was sick.

2. **acknowledge** (ak näl′ ij) admit to be true
   a. The experts reluctantly* **acknowledged** that their estimate* of food costs was not accurate.*
   b. District Attorney Hogan got the man to **acknowledge** that he had lied in court.
   c. "I hate living alone," the bachelor* **acknowledged.**

3. **justice** (jus′ tis) just conduct; fair dealing
   a. Daniel Webster abandoned* any hope for **justice** once he saw the jury.
   b. Our pledge* to the flag refers to "liberty and **justice** for all."
   c. The warden* acknowledged* that **justice** had not been served in my case.

4. **delinquent** (di ling′ kwənt) an offender; criminal; behind time
   a. The youthful **delinquent** tried to avoid* going to jail.
   b. All **delinquents** are banned* from the Student Council at school.
   c. If you are **delinquent** in paying your dues, you will be dropped from membership in the club.

5. **reject** (ri jekt′) refuse to take, use, believe, consider, grant, etc.
   a. Sylvester didn't try to evade* the draft because he knew the doctors would **reject** him once they saw the X-rays of his back.
   b. The reform* bill was unanimously* **rejected** by Congress.
   c. When his promotion was **rejected** by the newspaper owner, the editor* was thoroughly* bewildered.*

6. **deprive** (di prīv′) take away from by force
   a. The poor man was **deprived** of a variety* of things that money could buy.
   b. We were **deprived** of a good harvest* because of the lack* of rain.
   c. Living in a rural* area, Betsy was **deprived** of concerts and plays.

7. **spouse** (spous) husband or wife
   a. When a husband prospers* in his business, his **spouse** benefits also.
   b. The woman and her **spouse** relieved* each other throughout the night at their child's bedside.
   c. "May I bring my **spouse** to the office party?" Dorinda asked.

8. **vocation** (vō kā′ shən) occupation; business; profession; trade
   a. Red Smith's **vocation** was as a journalist* for the *Times.*
   b. One should try to pick an appropriate* **vocation** that is appropriate for him or her.
   c. If you are uneasy* in your **vocation,** you can never be happy.

9. **unstable** (un stā′ bəl) not firmly fixed; easily moved or overthrown
   a. An **unstable** person will panic* when he or she is in trouble.
   b. I could detect* that the drinking glass was **unstable** and about to fall.
   c. Cathy's balance became **unstable** because she was very weary.*

10. **homicide** (häm′ ə sīd) a killing of one human being by another; murder
    a. The police were baffled* as to who was responsible for the **homicide.**
    b. It took a crafty* person to get away with that **homicide.**
    c. News of the **homicide** quickly circulated* through our vicinity.*

11. **penalize** (pē′ nə līz) declare punishable by law or rule; set a penalty for
    a. The Detroit Lions were **penalized** fifteen yards for their rough play.
    b. We were **penalized** for not following tradition.*
    c. Mrs. Robins **penalized** us for doing the math problem in ink.

12. **beneficiary** (ben ə fish′ ē  ēr ē or ben ə fish′ ə ē) person who receives benefit
    a. I was the **beneficiary** of $8,000 when my grandfather died.
    b. When the paintings were sold, the millionaire's niece was the **beneficiary.**
    c. My brother was the **beneficiary** of excellent advice from his guidance counselor.

---

### A New Way to Treat Prisoners

The **warden** of a prison today will readily **acknowledge** the new trend in prison reform.* In an attempt to provide a different brand of **justice** for society's **delinquents,** officials now **reject** the idea that prison should completely **deprive** the convict of freedom. Thus, in some prisons inmates are allowed to leave the prison grounds to visit their **spouses** or to pursue* their **vocation.** Even the more **unstable** convict who may have committed **homicide** is not **penalized** as harshly* as before. The hope is that if persons emerge* from prison less defiant* than they do now, society will be the **beneficiary.**

---

**Which of the words studied in this lesson is suggested by the picture?**

**Place one of the new words in each of the blanks below.**

1. Wayne's parents yelled at him because he was known as a _____.
2. The courts will _____ you if you don't obey the law.
3. Are you satisfied with your _____ or are you thinking of getting a different job?
4. Five persons were being questioned by the police about the brutal* _____.
5. I _____ the fact that I received the tapes.
6. When Steve asked his girlfriend to marry him, he did not anticipate* that she would _____ him.
7. The _____ of the prison set up stricter rules.
8. Mrs. Fried's _____ came home weary* after each day's work.
9. It is often _____ persons who commit serious crimes.
10. Clara felt as if she had been _____ of the better things in life.
11. _____ was served when the villain* was put behind bars.
12. Joseph was the _____ of large sums of money from his uncle's insurance policy.

---

**Matching.** Match the 12 new words in Column I with the definitions in Column II.

| Column I | Column II |
|---|---|
| _____ 1. warden | a. murder |
| _____ 2. penalize | b. admit to be true |
| _____ 3. justice | c. person in charge of a prison |
| _____ 4. delinquent | d. not firmly fixed |
| _____ 5. vocation | e. take away from by force |
| _____ 6. spouse | f. a criminal |
| _____ 7. homicide | g. person who receives benefit |
| _____ 8. acknowledge | h. declare punishable by law or rule |
| _____ 9. unstable | i. husband or wife |
| _____ 10. beneficiary | j. occupation |
| _____ 11. reject | k. fair dealing |
| _____ 12. deprive | l. refuse to take, use, believe, grant, etc. |

---

**Spotlight on:** **beneficiary**—Except for Benedict Arnold, who did not treat his country well, all other words beginning with *bene* speak only of good, for that is what this prefix (a letter or letters attached at the beginning of a word) means. Here is a list of such "good" words: benefactor, beneficent, beneficial, benefit, benevolent, benign. In your reading, have you come across the letters N.B. in front of certain passages? The author is telling you to "note it well" (*nota bene*).

# Lesson 23

"In words as fashions the same rule will hold,
Alike fantastic if too new or old;
Be not the first by whom the new are tried,
Nor yet the last to lay the old aside."

Alexander Pope, *Essay on Criticism*

## Words To Learn This Week

reptile
rarely
forbid
logical
exhibit
proceed
precaution
extract
prior
embrace
valiant
partial

1. **reptile** (rep' təl) a cold blooded animal that creeps or crawls; snakes, lizards, turtles, alligators, and crocodiles
   a. The lizard is a **reptile** with a very slender* body.
   b. **Reptiles** are kept in the museum's large hall.
   c. A crocodile is a **reptile** that is more nimble* in the water than out of it.

2. **rarely** (rãr' lē) seldom; not often
   a. You **rarely** hear adults raving* about a movie they just saw.
   b. People are **rarely** frank* with each other.
   c. I **rarely** attend the annual* meetings of our family circle.

3. **forbid** (fər bid') order someone not to do something; make a rule against
   a. Spitting on the floor is **forbidden** in public places.
   b. The law **forbids** drunken drivers to handle their autos.
   c. I **forbid** you to enter the dense* jungle because of the peril* which awaits you there.

4. **logical** (loj' ə kəl) reasonable; reasonably expected
   a. It is **logical** to spend a minimum* on needless things.
   b. In order to keep your car running well, it is only **logical** that you lubricate* it regularly.
   c. I used a **logical** argument to persuade* Lester to leave.

5. **exhibit** (eg zib' it) display; show
   a. A million dollar microscope* is now on **exhibit** at our school.
   b. The bride and groom **exhibited** their many expensive* gifts.
   c. Kim frequently* **exhibited** her vast knowledge* of baseball before complete strangers.

6. **proceed** (prə sēd') go on after having stopped; move forward
   a. Only those with special cards can **proceed** into the pool area.
   b. When the actor was late, the show **proceeded** without him.
   c. The senator **proceeded** to denounce* those wholesalers* who would deprive* Americans of their quota* of beef.

7. **precaution** (prə kô' shən) measures taken beforehand; foresight
   a. Detectives used **precaution** before entering the bomb's vicinity.*
   b. We must take every **precaution** not to pollute* the air.
   c. Before igniting* the fire, the hunters took unusual **precaution.**

8. **extract** (eks trakt') pull out or draw out, usually with some effort
   a. Dr. Fogel **extracted** my tooth in an amateur* fashion.
   b. Chemists **extracted** the essential* vitamins from the grain.
   c. Spencer was ingenious* in **extracting** information from witnesses.

9. **prior** (prī' ər) coming before; earlier
   a. **Prior** to choosing his life's vocation,* Paul traveled to India.
   b. Myrna was unhappy **prior** to meeting her beau.*
   c. Samson had been a strong man **prior** to having his hair cut.

10. **embrace** (em brās') hug one another; a hug
    a. After having been rivals* for years, the two men **embraced.**
    b. When Ellen's spouse* approached,* she slipped out of Doug's **embrace.**
    c. The young girl was bewildered* when the stranger **embraced** her.

11. **valiant** (val' yənt) brave; courageous
    a. Robin Hood was **valiant** and faced his opponents* without fear.
    b. The **valiant** paratroopers led the invasion.

c. Grandma Joad had the ability* to be **valiant** when the need arose.
12. **partial** (pär′ shəl) not complete; not total
   a. We made a **partial** listing of the urgently* needed supplies.
   b. Macy's had a sale on a **partial** selection of its winter clothes.
   c. Using only a **partial** amount of his great speed, Jim Ryun surpassed* all the other runners.

---

*Read the following story to see how the new words are used in it.*

### Handling Poisonous Snakes

How do the Indian snake charmers handle those live poisonous **reptiles** without being poisoned? Visitors to the Hopi Indians **rarely** leave the reservation without asking. Because Indians **forbid** any white person from taking part in such a ceremony, scientists could come to one **logical** answer: before the Indians **exhibit** the snakes, they **proceed** to remove the fangs. Yet some scientists verify* the fact that all the snakes have fangs. They have a different theory.* The Indians take an important **precaution:** they **extract** most of the poison **prior** to the snake dance. Now the Indian can **embrace** the snake without being poisoned. He will appear **valiant** because he knows that the snake has only a **partial** supply of its deadly poison.

---

**Which of the words studied in this lesson is suggested by the picture?**

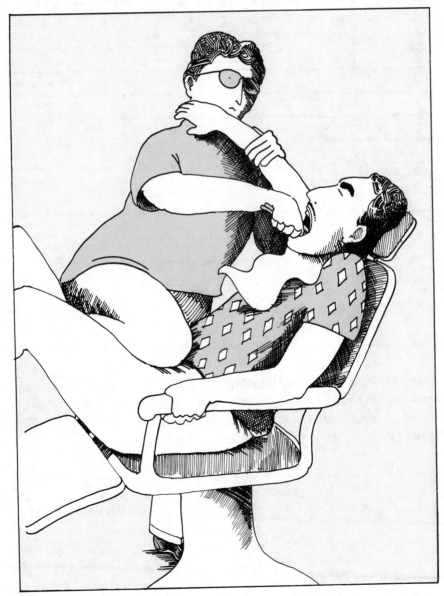

**Place one of the new words in each of the blanks below.**

1.  I _____ my daughter when she came home from camp.
2.  We _____ you to leave the area.
3.  Did you _____ along the hall until you got to the room?
4.  A turtle is a very common _____.
5.  We made a _____ listing of the people who owed the library books because it would take too long to copy all the names.
6.  Betty Sue is always very _____ when she prepares her arguments for a debate.*
7.  I _____ if ever go to the movies.
8.  Have you seen the cave dweller_____in the museum?
9.  I went to high school _____ to entering the army.
10. Be sure to take the _____ not to swim after eating.
11. Sergeant York got a medal for being _____ in war.
12. Did you _____ the splinter from his foot?

---

**Exercise**

*Now make up your own sentences, one for each of the new words you have just been taught.*

1. _____
2. _____
3. _____
4. _____
5. _____
6. _____
7. _____
8. _____
9. _____
10. _____
11. _____
12. _____

---

**Spotlight on:**    **valiant**—The famous Prince Valiant has appeared in the comics for many years as the ideal knight. Since English has so many synonyms for the quality of courage, he might have been called Prince Gallant, Intrepid, Audacious, Hardy, Resolute, Indomitable, Fearless, Dauntless, Chivalrous, or Heroic. Or was Prince Valiant just the right name?

# Lesson 24

"Words are the physicians of a mind diseased."

Aeschylus, *Prometheus Bound*

**Words To Learn This Week**

fierce
detest
sneer
scowl
encourage
consider
vermin
wail
symbol
authority
neutral
trifle

1. **fierce** (fērs) savage; wild
   a. Barry was so **fiercely** angry that he thrust* his hand through the glass.
   b. One must take appropriate* precautions* when approaching* **fierce** dogs.
   c. He took one look at his **fierce** opponent* and ran.

2. **detest** (di test') dislike very much; hate
   a. The world **detests** people who aren't valiant.*
   b. Wally was certain that his girlfriend's parents would **detest** him because he had been a delinquent.*
   c. I **detest** Chinese food but I won't deprive* you of the chance to eat it.

3. **sneer** (snēr) show scorn or contempt by looks or words; a scornful look or remark
   a. The journalists* were cautious* about **sneering** at the Secretary of Defense.
   b. "Wipe that **sneer** off your face!" the dean told the delinquent.*
   c. When offered a dime as a tip, the taxi driver **sneered** at his rider.

4. **scowl** (skoul) look angry by lowering the eyebrows; frown
   a. Laverne **scowled** at her mother when she was prohibited* from going out.
   b. I dread* seeing my father **scowl** when he gets my report card.
   c. Because of a defect* in her vision,* it always appeared that Polly was **scowling.**

5. **encourage** (en kər' ij) give courage to; increase the confidence of
   a. We **encouraged** the coach to devise* a plan for beating Jefferson High.
   b. Some unstable* persons need to be **encouraged** to find a vocation.*
   c. A valiant* person rarely* needs to be **encouraged.**

6. **consider** (kən sid' ər) think about in order to decide
   a. Jon **considered** whether a comprehensive* report was necessary.
   b. Do you **consider** that dress to be a bargain at the wholesale* price?
   c. The wrestler was always **considered** to be the underdog* in every match.

7. **vermin** (ver' mən) small animals that are troublesome or destructive; fleas, bedbugs, lice, rats, and mice are vermin
   a. One should try to eliminate* all **vermin** from his or her house.
   b. Some reptiles* eat **vermin** as their food.
   c. Although **vermin** are not always visible,* they probably inhabit* every house in the city.

8. **wail** (wāl) cry loud and long because of grief or pain
   a. When tragedy* struck, the old people began to **wail.**
   b. In some countries the women are expected to **wail** loudly after their husbands die.
   c. When the Yankees lost the World Series, there was much **wailing** in New York.

9. **symbol** (sim' bəl) something that stands for or represents something else
   a. The statue outside the court building is considered* a **symbol** of justice.*
   b. **Symbols** for God are prohibited* in the Jewish religion.
   c. An olive branch is a **symbol** of peace.

10. **authority** (e thôr' e tē, e thär' e tē) the right to command or enforce obedience; power delegated to another; an author or volume that may be appealed to in support of an action or belief
    a. No one should have the **authority** to dictate our career choice.
    b. Today a monarch* does not have the **authority** he once enjoyed.
    c. The Supreme Court is entrusted with the **authority** to interpret our Constitution.

73

11.  **neutral** (nōo′ trəl) on neither side of a quarrel or war
    a.   It is logical* to remain **neutral** in a violent* argument between spouses.*
    b.   Switzerland was a **neutral** country in World War II.
    c.   Adolph did not reject* the idea but remained **neutral** about it.
12.  **trifle** (trī′ fəl) a small amount; little bit; something of little value
    a.   I ate a **trifle** for dinner rather than a vast* meal.
    b.   Walter spends only a **trifle** of his time in studying French.
    c.   At our meetings Alex always raises **trifling** objections to any new plan.

## Punishment for Drug Abuse

A recent* attempt by New Jersey's attorney general to lessen the penalties* for use of marijuana has caused **fierce** arguments around the country. Those who **detest** the drug users **sneer** and **scowl** at the light treatment of offenders. They reject* the attorney general's recommendation as lacking a morsel* of sense, claiming it would only **encourage** more drug abuse. They **consider** the drug addict much like **vermin** that must be stamped out.

Such citizens continually **wail** for stiffer penalties. Those in favor of a milder approach* to the drug problem point to the poor results achieved by prison terms. They feel addicts* should be given medical help. Also, in enforcing harsh* drug laws, police tend to be viewed as a **symbol** of unwelcome **authority.** The problem demands a solution. We cannot remain **neutral** or unconcerned, nor can we afford to muddle through with ineffective measures, for this is not a **trifling** matter.

**Which of the words studied in this lesson is suggested by the picture?**

**Place one of the new words in each of the blanks below.**

1.  I have it on the highest _____ that the lead in the play has been chosen.
2.  I am going to _____ my brother to become a lawyer.
3.  Uncle Sam is the well-known _____ of the United States.
4.  We pay $5 a month to keep our house free from _____.
5.  When a country is _____, it does not want to get involved in foreign conflict.*
6.  What type of art work do you _____ to be beautiful?
7.  The _____ lion clawed at the visitors to the zoo.
8.  To hear the _____ of a person in sorrow is to hear a dismal* sound.
9.  Only a _____ of Ivan's fortune was left to his human beneficiaries;* most of the money was given to his cats.
10.  I _____ people who are jealous* of my success.
11.  The unpleasant salesgirl always had a _____ on her face.
12.  My father warned me not to _____ at our poor relatives.


**Synonyms.** Circle the word that most nearly expresses the meaning of the word printed in heavy black type.

1.  **encourage**
    a.  evade*
    b.  approach*
    c.  reassure
    d.  cuddle

2.  **neutral**
    a.  impartial
    b.  reckless
    c.  abundant*
    d.  bulky

3.  **scowl**
    a.  alter*
    b.  forbid*
    c.  frown
    d.  complicate

4.  **consider**
    a.  think over
    b.  assume responsibility
    c.  issue orders
    d.  accept a challenge*

5.  **fierce**
    a.  massive*
    b.  sinister*
    c.  savage
    d.  coarse

6.  **detest**
    a.  abolish*
    b.  hate
    c.  baffle*
    d.  ignore*

7.  **authority**
    a.  opinion
    b.  valuable skill
    c.  deciding factor
    d.  power to act

8.  **symbol**
    a.  image
    b.  concealed* evidence*
    c.  absurdity*
    d.  sacred* object

9.  **trifle**
    a.  fragile* glass
    b.  flexible* hours
    c.  small amount
    d.  ignorant statement

10.  **vermin**
    a.  small and troublesome animals
    b.  boring and disappointing movies
    c.  curious readers
    d.  crafty* clients*

11.  **sneer**
    a.  scornful look
    b.  gallant* gesture
    c.  sinister* act
    d.  rude interruption

12.  **wail**
    a.  calm down
    b.  cry loud and long
    c.  go forward
    d.  break even

---

**Spotlight on:**    **symbol**—Our civilization is quite dependent upon symbols. Without them, the world would be drab and dull indeed. The very words we use are merely symbols for the things and ideas they represent. Symbols are used in language, writing, logic, mathematics, science, religion, trade, and sports. Find a symbol for each of the fields mentioned.

# Word Review #4

These exercises are based on some of the words which you found in Lessons 19–24.

**A.** In each of the parentheses below there are two choices. Pick the one that fits better.

1. In order to help our own auto companies, the government set up (quotas, estimates) on the number of foreign cars it would allow to be sent here.
2. To make sure that our sauce is good, we hire workers to (harvest, reject) those tomatoes that are not ripe.
3. My hopes for visiting Canada this summer hang on a (fragile, logical) thread.
4. Try to (extract, acknowledge) every ounce of juice you can get from these oranges.
5. When I need help with a (dilemma, trifle), I turn to my father who always gives me good advice.
6. Since you have made (partial, abundant) payment for your bicycle, you still owe quite a few dollars.
7. If you (linger, proceed) too long over your breakfast, you will be late for school.
8. I didn't want to get mixed up in the fight between Luke and Pete, so I took a (neutral, defiant) position.
9. Once I had (calculated, exhibited) how long it would take to do the jobs, I knew what to charge.
10. After the facts were (confirmed, relieved), the editor* printed the story.

**B. Opposites.** In Column I are ten words from Lessons 19–24. Match them correctly with their *opposite* meanings in Column II.

| Column I | Column II |
|---|---|
| 1. detest | a. huge piece |
| 2. perish | b. hide |
| 3. valiant | c. wide awake |
| 4. emerge | d. afraid |
| 5. unstable | e. afterwards |
| 6. weary | f. be fond of |
| 7. scowl | g. often |
| 8. prior | h. live |
| 9. morsel | i. smile |
| 10. rarely | j. steady |

**C.** Which of the vocabulary choices in parentheses fits best in these newspaper headlines?

1. **Egyptian Art _____ To Open At Local Museum**    (Quota, Exhibit, Extract, Symbol)
2. **Middle East Countries To Test _____ Peace**    (Fragile, Appropriate, Prior, Neutral)
3. **Trucks _____ In Highway Accident**    (Proceed, Linger, Collide, Detour)
4. **Ask Retired Judge To Solve _____**    (Threat, Panic, Plea, Dilemma)
5. **Slum Houses To Be Rid Of _____**    (Vermin, Merit, Reptiles, Vigor)
6. **Police _____ Arrest Of Jewelry Thief**    (Transmit, Merit, Extract, Confirm)
7. **New Arrivals Hope to _____ In America**    (Prosper, Verify, Emerge, Ban)
8. **Family Pets _____ In Four-Alarm Fire**    (Partial, Perish, Scowl, Devour)
9. **"Must Meet _____," Salesmen Are Told**    (Beneficiary, Quota, Threat, Merit)
10. **Farmers Pleased With _____ Crop**    (Logical, Uneasy, Abundant, Jagged)

**D.** From the list of words below choose the word that means:

1. a trap from which to make a surprise attack *and* is a simpler word for *ambuscade*
2. the person to be paid money from an insurance policy *and* begins with the prefix meaning "good"
3. a letter, character, mark, sign or abbreviation *that* represents an idea or quality
4. the end product of a farmer's work *but also* refers to the product of any toil or effort
5. alarm *and* is derived from the name of the Greek god who brought fear whenever he appeared
6. succeed *and also* attain one's desires
7. defeat *as well as* perplex or puzzle
8. the chief officer of a prison *and also* a guardian or a superintendent
9. taking care beforehand *as well as* provision for an emergency
10. something of little value or importance *and also* to play with or treat lightly someone's feelings

| | | | | | |
|---|---|---|---|---|---|
| wail | precaution | symbol | collide | merit | absorb |
| quota | beneficiary | baffle | verify | jagged | devour |
| proceed | acknowledge | prior | ambush | crafty | trifle |
| penalize | appropriate | deprive | panic | prosper | warden |
| harvest | transmit | plea | anticipate | defiant | vigor |

# Lesson 25

## Words To Learn This Week

architect
matrimony
baggage
squander
abroad
fugitive
calamity
pauper
envy
collapse
prosecute
bigamy

1. **architect** (är' kə tekt) a person who makes plans for buildings and other structures; a maker; a creator
   a. The famous **architect,** Frank Lloyd Wright, designed his buildings to blend* with their surroundings.
   b. An **architect** must have a knowledge of the materials that will be used in his structures.
   c. General Eisenhower was the **architect** of victory over the Nazis in World War II.

2. **matrimony** (mat' rə mō' nē) married life; ceremony of marriage
   a. Though **matrimony** is a holy state, our local governments still collect a fee for the marriage license.
   b. Because of lack of money, the sweetness of their **matrimony** turned sour.
   c. Some bachelors* find it very difficult to give up their freedom for the blessings of **matrimony.**

3. **baggage** (bag' ij) the trunks and suitcases a person takes when he or she travels; an army's equipment
   a. When Walt unpacked his **baggage,** he found he had forgotten his radio.
   b. Mrs. Montez checked her **baggage** at the station and took the children for a walk.
   c. The modern army cannot afford to be slowed up with heavy **baggage.**

4. **squander** (skwän' dər) spend foolishly; waste
   a. Do not **squander** your money by buying what you cannot use.
   b. Because Freddy **squandered** his time watching television, he could not catch up on his homework.
   c. In his will, Mr. Larson warned his children not to **squander** their inheritance.

5. **abroad** (a brôd') outside one's country; going around; far and wide
   a. More people are going **abroad** for vacations.
   b. Is there any truth to the rumor **abroad** that school will be open all summer?
   c. The news of the President's illness spread **abroad.**

6. **fugitive** (fyo͞o ' jə tiv) a runaway
   a. Paul was a **fugitive** from the slums, abandoned* by all his friends.
   b. After escaping from prison, Tom led an unhappy life as a **fugitive** from the law.
   c. The **fugitives** from the unsuccessful revolution were captured.

7. **calamity** (kə lam' ə tē) a great misfortune; serious trouble
   a. Failure in one test should not be regarded as a **calamity.**
   b. The death of her husband was a **calamity** which left Mrs. Marlowe numb.*
   c. What is more dismal* than one **calamity** following upon the heels of another?

8. **pauper** (pô' pər) a very poor person
   a. The fire that destroyed his factory made Mr. Bloomson a **pauper.**
   b. The richest man is a **pauper** if he has no friends.
   c. Since he was once a **pauper** himself, Max is willing to help the needy whenever he can.

9. **envy** (en' vē) jealousy; the object of jealousy; to feel jealous
   a. Marilyn's selection as Prom Queen made her the **envy** of every senior.
   b. My parents taught me not to **envy** anyone else's wealth.
   c. Our **envy** of Nora's skating ability is foolish because with practice all of us could do as well.

10. **collapse** (kə laps′) a breakdown; to fall in; break down; fail suddenly; fold together
    a. A heavy flood caused the bridge to **collapse.**
    b. His failure in chemistry meant the **collapse** of Bob's summer plans.
    c. **Collapse** the trays and store them in the closet.
11. **prosecute** (präs′ ə ko͞ot) bring before a court; follow up; carry on
    a. Drunken drivers should be **prosecuted.**
    b. The district attorney refused to **prosecute** the case for lack of evidence.
    c. The general **prosecuted** the war with vigor.*
12. **bigamy** (big′ ə mē) having two wives or two husbands at the same time
    a. Some people look upon **bigamy** as double trouble.
    b. Mr. Winkle, looking at his wife, thought **bigamy** was one crime he would never be guilty of.
    c. Some religious groups are in favor of **bigamy** even though it is against the law of the land.

---

*Read the following story to see how the new words are used in it.*

**Love and Marriage**

The famous **architect** Melville Fenton grew tired of **matrimony** and devised* a scheme to free himself of his spouse.* He told her he had been engaged by an American company to design its new office building in Paris. Packing his **baggage,** he left his home and proceeded* to cut all his ties with his former life. He changed his name, secured a new job, and quickly forgot his faithful wife.

Not having any responsibilities, he began to **squander** his money and energy. He married another woman, believing he was safe from the law. But his first wife had grown suspicious and resentful.* She learned from his employer that he had not gone **abroad,** that in fact he had left the firm altogether. With a little detective work, she soon discovered her husband's whereabouts. He had become a **fugitive** from justice* and one **calamity** after another overtook him. He lost his job, became a **pauper** and was no longer the **envy** of his acquaintances. Then his second wife grew ill and died.

After the **collapse** of his plans, there was only one logical* step for Melville to take. He embraced* his wife and asked for her forgiveness. Much to his relief, she decided not to **prosecute** him for **bigamy.**

---

**Place one of the new words in each of the blanks below.**

1. The _____ compartment of the plane was inspected for bombs.
2. A storm on the night of the prom meant _____ for the senior class plans.
3. Good government would assure that there are no more _____ in the land.
4. The strain of the three-hour examination almost brought Leslie to a state of_____.
5. Now that the quintuplets have come along, we are calling on an _____ to devise* plans for an extension to our home.
6. The hungry man was _____ for stealing a loaf of bread.
7. Bringing expensive* toys to newborn infants is just another way to_____ your money.
8. Bloodhounds were brought in to hunt for the _____ in the dense* forest.
9. When it was learned that Mr. Smythe had failed to divorce his first wife, he was charged with _____.
10. Traveling _____ is an educational experience.
11. What is there to _____ in a high mark that was not honestly achieved?
12. Everyone can see that _____ has brought Jim and Stella great happiness.

---

**Exercise**

*Now make up your own sentences, one for each of the new words you have just been taught.*

1. _____

2. _____

3. _____

4. _____

5. _____

6. _____

7. _____

8. _____

9. _____

10. _____

11. _____

12. _____

**Which of the words studied in this lesson is suggested by the picture?**

**Spotlight on:**    **architect**—The architect is only the first of many workers needed before a building is completed. Some others are engineers, bulldozer operators, welders, carpenters, masons, lathers, plumbers, electricians, roofers, painters, plasterers, tilers, glaziers. Of course, you might simply hire a contractor who would then have all the headaches.

# Lesson 26

"What do you read, my Lord?"
"Words, words, words."

Shakespeare, *Hamlet*

**Words To Learn This Week**

possible
compel
awkward
venture
awesome
guide
quench
betray
utter
pacify
respond
beckon

1. **possible** (päs′ ə bl) able to be, be done, or happen; able to be true; able to be done or chosen properly
   a. Call me tomorrow evening if **possible.**
   b. It is now **possible** for man to walk on the moon.
   c. Considering* Melissa's weakness in writing, it is not **possible** for her to help you with your composition.

2. **compel** (kəm pel′) force; get by force
   a. It is not possible* to **compel** a person to love his fellow man.
   b. Heavy floods **compelled** us to stop.
   c. Mr. Gorlin is a teacher who does not have to **compel** me to behave.

3. **awkward** (ô′ kwərd) clumsy; not well-suited to use; not easily managed; embarrassing
   a. Sally is very **awkward** in speaking to the class but quite relaxed with her own group of friends.
   b. The handle of this bulky* suitcase has an **awkward** shape.
   c. Slow down because this is an **awkward** corner to turn.

4. **venture** (ven′ chər) a daring undertaking; an attempt to make money by taking business risks; to dare; to expose to risk
   a. Ulysses was a man who would not reject* any **venture,** no matter how dangerous.
   b. John Jacob Astor made his fortune by a lucky **venture** in animal furs.
   c. Medics **venture** their lives to save wounded soldiers.

5. **awesome** (ô′ səm) causing or showing great fear, wonder, or respect
   a. The towering mountains, covered with snow, are an **awesome** sight.
   b. Connie had such an **awesome** amount of work to complete before graduation she doubted* she would have everything ready in time.
   c. The atom bomb is an **awesome** achievement for mankind.

6. **guide** (gid) a person who shows the way; to direct; to manage
   a. Tourists often hire **guides.**
   b. The Indian **guided** the hunters through the forest.
   c. Use the suggestions in the handbook as a study **guide.**

7. **quench** (kwench) put an end to; drown or put out
   a. Foam will **quench** an oil fire.
   b. Only Pepsi Cola will **quench** my thirst on such a hot day.
   c. He reads and reads and reads to **quench** his thirst for knowledge.

8. **betray** (bitrā′) give away to the enemy; be unfaithful; mislead; show
   a. Nick's awkward* motions **betrayed** his nervousness.
   b. Without realizing what he was doing, the talkative soldier **betrayed** his unit's plans.
   c. The child's eyes **betrayed** his fear of the fierce* dog.

9. **utter** (ut′ ər) speak; make known; express
   a. When Violet accidentally stepped on the nail, she **uttered** a sharp cry of pain.
   b. Seth was surprised when he was told that he had **uttered** Joan's name in his sleep.
   c. When Mr. Fuller saw that his house had not been damaged in the fire, he **uttered** a sigh of relief.*

10. **pacify** (pas′ ə fī) make calm; quiet down; bring peace to
   a. This toy should **pacify** that screaming baby.

   b.  We tried to **pacify** the woman who was angry at having to wait so long in line.
   c.  Soldiers were sent to **pacify** the countryside.

11. **respond** (ri spänd′) answer; react
   a.  Greg **responded** quickly to the question.
   b.  My dog **responds** to every command I give him.
   c.  Mrs. Cole **responded** to the medicine so well that she was better in two days.

12. **beckon** (bek′ ən) signal by a motion of the hand or head; attract
   a.  Jack **beckoned** to me to follow him.
   b.  The delicious smell of fresh bread **beckoned** the hungry boy.
   c.  The sea **beckons** us to adventure.

---

*Read the following story to see how the new words are used in it.*

### Some Tall Tales

Do you think it is **possible** to defeat an opponent so fierce* that a glance* at her turns one to stone? This was the fate of anyone who looked upon the Medusa, a dreaded* monster whose hair was made of hissing serpents. The brave Perseus undertook to fight the Medusa, but he was **compelled** to do battle in a most **awkward** manner. To help Perseus in his **venture,** the goddess Minerva had lent him her bright shield, and the god Mercury had given him winged shoes. Cautiously he approached the **awesome** monster. Using the image of the Medusa in his shield as a **guide,** he succeeded in cutting off her head and fixing it to the center of Minerva's shield.

Perseus then flew to the realm of King Atlas whose chief pride was his garden filled with golden fruit. Thirsty and near collapse,* he pleaded with the king for water to **quench** his thirst and for a place to rest. But Atlas feared that he would be **betrayed** into losing his golden apples. He **uttered** just one word, "Begone!" Perseus, finding that he could not **pacify** Atlas, **responded** by **beckoning** him to look upon Medusa's head. Atlas was changed immediately into stone. His head and hair became forests, his body increased in bulk and became cliffs, and the gods ruled that the heaven with all its stars should rest upon his shoulders. Can there be a worse calamity* than that which befell Atlas?

---

### Which of the words studied in this lesson is suggested by the picture?

**Place one of the new words in each of the blanks below.**

1.  History has shown us that tyranny* cannot_____the human desire for freedom.
2.  The sailors used the North Star to _____ them to their destination.
3.  Our eyes _____ to sudden light by blinking.
4.  The coach _____ to the pitcher to watch for a bunt.
5.  Little Benjy was foolish enough to _____ out on the thin ice.
6.  If we are _____ to vote without hearing all sides of the issue, we could make a serious mistake.
7.  Power in the hands of the ignorant is an _____ responsibility.
8.  Benedict Arnold _____ his country.
9.  The only _____ excuse for Barry's failure is his lack* of effort.
10. It was not possible* to _____ the excited woman after she was fined for jaywalking.
11. The last words _____ by the dying soldier were, "We must hold the fort."
12. Ralph found himself in an _____ situation when his blind date turned out to be a foot taller than he.

---

**True or False.** Based on the way the new word is used, write T (true) or F (false) next to the sentence.

_____  1. An **awkward** person is very graceful.
_____  2. An **awesome** sight is one that causes great wonder and respect.
_____  3. If someone tells you it's **possible** to do something, that means the thing cannot be done.
_____  4. To **beckon** is to signal by a motion of the hand or head to call someone over to you.
_____  5. A person who shows you the way is a **guide.**
_____  6. To **utter** is to remain silent.
_____  7. To quiet an angry mob is to **pacify** the crowd.
_____  8. If you are **compelled** to do something, your are forced to do it.
_____  9. A person who undertakes a **venture** is afraid to take risks of any kind.
_____  10. If I **respond** to your suggestion, I react to it.
_____  11. To **quench** something is to renew it.
_____  12. To **betray** someone is to be unfaithful or misleading.

---

**Spotlight on:**   **respond** — The next time you receive an invitation to a party, the host or hostess may want to be sure you are coming so that adequate preparations can be made. In that case, he or she will write R.S.V.P. on the invitation to tell you in simple French (*répondez s'il vous plaît*) to please respond.

# Lesson 27

"My words fly up, my thoughts remain below:
Words without thoughts never to heaven go."

Shakespeare, *Hamlet*

## Words To Learn This Week

despite
disrupt
rash
rapid
exhaust
severity
feeble
unite
cease
thrifty
miserly
monarch

1. **despite** (di spit') in spite of
   a. The player continued in the game **despite** his injuries.
   b. **Despite** his size, Ted put up a good fight.
   c. We won the game by a shutout **despite** the fact that our team got only three hits.

2. **disrupt** (dis rupt') upset; cause to break down
   a. Pam's clowning **disrupted** the class every day.
   b. The storm **disrupted** the telephone lines throughout the area.
   c. The collapse* of the government **disrupted** the services we took for granted, such as mail delivery.

3. **rash** (rash) a breaking out with many small red spots on the skin; outbreak of many instances within a short time; too hasty or careless
   a. The report of a **rash** of burglaries in the neighborhood was exaggerated.*
   b. Poison ivy causes a **rash.**
   c. It is **rash** to threaten an action you cannot carry out.

4. **rapid** (ra' pid) very quick; swift
   a. We took a **rapid** walk around the camp before breakfast.
   b. If you work **rapidly** you can complete the test in twenty minutes.
   c. The response* to the surprise attack was a **rapid** retreat.

5. **exhaust** (ig zôst') empty completely; use up; tire out
   a. To **exhaust** the city's water supply would be a calamity.*
   b. The long climb to the top of the mountain **exhausted** our strength.
   c. If we continue to squander* our money recklessly,* our treasury will soon be **exhausted.**

6. **severity** (sə ver' ə tē) strictness; harshness; plainness; violence
   a. The **severity** of the teacher was not appreciated by the pupils until they reached the final examinations
   b. The **severity** of the Black Plague can be imagined from the fact that thirty percent of the population* died.
   c. Rosita complained to the principal about the **severity** of the punishment which the Student Court gave to her.

7. **feeble** (fē' bl) weak
   a. We heard a **feeble** cry from the exhausted* child.
   b. The guide* made a **feeble** attempt to explain why he had taken the wrong turn.
   c. The **feeble** old man collapsed* on the sidewalk.

8. **unite** (yu̇ nīt') join together; become one
   a. The thirteen colonies **united** to form one country.
   b. Matrimony* **united** two famous Virginia families.
   c. America and Russia were **united** against a common enemy in World War II.

9. **cease** (sēs) stop
   a. **Cease** trying to do more than you can.
   b. The whispering in the audience **ceased** when the curtain went up.
   c. When you **cease** making war, you can then begin to pacify* the small villages which the enemy controls.

10. **thrifty** (thrif' tē) saving; careful in spending; thriving
    a. By being **thrifty,** Miss Benson managed to get along on her small income.

    b.  A **thrifty** person knows that squandering\* money can lead to financial\* calamity.\*

    c.  By **thrifty** use of their supplies, the shipwrecked sailors were able to survive\* for weeks.

11.   **miserly** (mī′ zər lē) stingy; like a miser

    a.  Being **miserly** with our natural resources will help us to live longer on this earth.

    b.  A **miserly** person rarely\* has any friends.

    c.  Silas Marner abandoned\* his **miserly** habits when Eppie came into his life.

12.   **monarch** (män′ ərk) king or queen; ruler

    a.  There are few modern nations which are governed by **monarchs.**

    b.  The **monarchs** of ancient Rome considered themselves descendants\* of the gods.

    c.  Men sometimes believe that they are **monarchs** in their own homes.

---

*Read the following story to see how the new words are used in it.*

### Problems We Face

**Despite** wars, disease, and natural disasters,\* our world is experiencing a population explosion (boom) that threatens\* to change or **disrupt** life as we have known it. Vast\* numbers of people must be fed and housed, and in the process a whole **rash** of problems has descended\* upon the human race.

First has been the pollution\* of the air and the contamination\* of the water supply. Second has been the **rapid exhaustion** of fuels, minerals, and other natural resources. The response\* to this situation has ranged from utter\* disbelief to exaggerated\* concern.

Since scientists themselves disagree on the **severity** of the problem, our **feeble** knowledge is surely unable to suggest the correct course of action. But we cannot stand still because there is too much at stake. We are, therefore, compelled\* to **unite** in our efforts to insure that human life on this planet does not **cease.** We must learn to be **thrifty,** even **miserly,** with the gifts of nature that we have formerly taken for granted. If our past reveals\* a reckless\* squandering\* of our natural possessions, we must now find an intelligent guide\* to their use so that we may remain **monarchs** of a world that has peace and plenty.

---

**Which of the words studied in this lesson is suggested by the picture?**

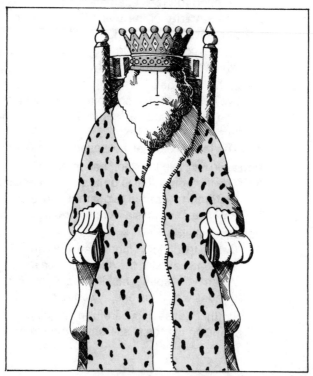

**Place one of the new words in each of the blanks below.**

1. The dying soldier made a last _____ effort to rise.
2. Though the victim's breathing had _____, the fireman continued giving oxygen.
3. We often regret a _____ statement made in the heat of an argument.
4. Now that you have _____ all your excuses, tell us the truth.
5. The bout was fought to determine who would be the_____ of the ring.
6. An increase in pollution* will _____ our normal ways of life.
7. Macy's Department Store always says, "It pays to be _____."
8. I have learned to read Spanish _____, but I cannot speak it so well.
9. The _____ of the pain compelled* Frank to call the doctor in the middle of the night.
10. Under certain conditions, oxygen will _____ with hydrogen to form water.
11. _____ a warning glance from the teacher, Harold continued to annoy the girl next to him.
12. It is best to be neither too _____ nor too careless about one's money.

___

**Exercise**

*Now make up your own sentences, one for each of the new words you have just been taught.*

1. _____
2. _____
3. _____
4. _____
5. _____
6. _____
7. _____
8. _____
9. _____
10. _____
11. _____
12. _____

___

**Spotlight on:**     **thrifty** — If a person is very thrifty with money, would you describe him or her as economical or stingy, careful or miserly, frugal or greedy? Though the trait is the same in each case, the word describing it has a different value judgment. The word you choose really depends upon what you think of the person.

# Lesson 28

"A fine volley of words, gentlemen, and quickly shot off."

Shakespeare, *Two Gentlemen of Verona*

1. **outlaw** (out′ lô) an exile; an outcast; a criminal; to declare unlawful
   a. Congress has **outlawed** the sale of certain drugs.
   b. The best known **outlaw** of the American West was Jesse James.
   c. An animal which is cast out by the rest of the pack is known as an **outlaw.**

2. **promote** (prə mōt′) raise in rank or importance; help to grow and develop; help to organize
   a. Students who pass the test will be **promoted** to the next grade.
   b. An accurate* knowledge of other cultures will **promote** good will among people of different backgrounds.
   c. Several bankers invested an enormous* sum of money to **promote** the idea.

3. **undernourished** (un′ dər ner′ isht) not sufficiently fed
   a. The **undernourished** child was so feeble* he could hardly walk.
   b. There is evidence* that even wealthy people are **undernourished** because they do not eat sufficient quantities* of healthful foods.
   c. An infant who drinks enough milk will not be **undernourished.**

4. **illustrate** (il′ əs trāt or i lus′ trat) make clear or explain by stories, examples, comparisons, or other means; serve as an example
   a. To **illustrate** how the heart sends blood around the body, the teacher described how a pump works.
   b. This exhibit* will **illustrate** the many uses of atomic energy.
   c. These stories **illustrate** Mark Twain's serious side.

5. **disclose** (dis klōz′) uncover; make known
   a. The lifting of the curtain **disclosed** a beautiful winter scene.
   b. This letter **discloses** the source* of his fortune.
   c. Samson, reclining* in the arms of Delilah, **disclosed** that the secret of his strength was in his long hair.

6. **excessive** (ek ses′ iv) too much; too great; extreme
   a. Pollution* of the atmosphere is an **excessive** price to pay for so-called progress.
   b. Numerous* attempts have been made to outlaw* jet planes that make **excessive** noise.
   c. The inhabitants* of Arizona are unaccustomed* to **excessive** rain.

7. **disaster** (də zas′ tər) an event that causes much suffering or loss; a great misfortune
   a. The hurricane's violent* winds brought **disaster** to the coastal town.
   b. The San Francisco earthquake and the Chicago fire are two of the greatest **disasters** in American history.
   c. The coach considered* the captain's injury a **disaster** for the team.

8. **censor** (sen′ sər) person who tells others how they ought to behave; one who changes books, plays and other works so as to make them acceptable to the government; to make changes in
   a. Some governments, national and local, **censor** books.
   b. The **censor** felt that fiction* as well as other books should receive the stamp of approval before they were put on sale.
   c. Any mention of the former prime minister was outlawed* by the **censor.**

9. **culprit** (kul′ prit) offender; person guilty of a fault or crime
   a. Who is the **culprit** who has eaten all the strawberries?
   b. The police caught the **culprit** with the stolen articles in his car.
   c. In the Sherlock Holmes story, the **culprit** turned out to be a snake.

10. **juvenile** (jo͞o′ və nīl or jo͞o′ və nl) young; youthful; of or for boys and girls; a young person
    a. My sister is known in the family as a **juvenile** delinquent.*
    b. Paula is still young enough to wear **juvenile** fashions.
    c. Ellen used to devour* "Cinderella" and other stories for **juveniles.**

11. **bait** (bāt) anything, especially food, used to attract fish or other animals so that they may be caught; anything used to tempt or attract a person to begin something he or she does not wish to do; to put bait on (a hook) or in (a trap); torment by unkind or annoying remarks
    a. The secret of successful trout fishing is finding the right **bait.**
    b. How can you expect to **bait** Mike into running for the class presidency when he has already refused every appeal?*
    c. Eddie is a good hunter because he knows the merit* of each kind of **bait** for the different animals.

12. **insist** (in sist′) keep firmly to some demand, statement, or position
    a. Mother **insists** that we do our homework before we start the long telephone conversations.
    b. She **insisted** that Sal was not jealous* of his twin brother.
    c. The doctor **insisted** that Marian get plenty of rest after the operation.

---

*Read the following story to see how the new words are used in it.*

### What Did You Have for Breakfast?

A parents' organization to protect children's health appealed* to a Senate committee to **outlaw** television commercials that **promote** the purchase of sugary products. Too much advertising urges the young child to eat caramels, chocolate, cookies, and pastries. This results in poor eating habits and leaves youngsters **undernourished** and subject to rapid* tooth decay and other diseases.

To **illustrate** the extent of the problem, a recent survey of one typical* day of CBS's Channel 7 in Boston between 7 A.M. and 2 P.M. **disclosed** 67 commercials for sweet-tasting products. Several witnesses said that many children's cereals contained more than 50 percent sugar, that children often forced their parents to buy the cereals, and that **excessive** use of sugar from cereals,

soft drinks and snack foods is a national **disaster.** Dr. Jean Mayer, professor of nutrition at Harvard University, recommended **censoring** the **culprits** in advertising for **juvenile** viewers. Recognizing the powerful opponents* in the food industry who will resist* control, Dr. Mayer said that no feeble* efforts will do. "Sugar-coated nothings," he added, "must cease* to be the standard diet of the American child."

Other witnesses pointed out that many cereal boxes used as **bait** for the children offers of dolls, balloons, airplane or car models, magic kits, monster cutouts and similar trifles,* but the cereal inside the box, they **insisted,** had no more food value than the container it came in.

---

### Place one of the new words in each of the blanks below.

1. The average American can be considered*_____because he or she deprives* the body of proper foods in favor of rich, fatty foods.

2. Though he was threatened* with imprisonment, Martin would not _____ the whereabouts of the treasure.

3. When the report of the airplane _____ reached us, many people pledged* their help in locating* survivors.*

4. The only hope for the world is to _____ war.

5. The police were reluctant* to use_____force, even to preserve* order.

6. This is a court of justice* for the _____ and the innocent alike.

7. Certain foods that _____ tooth decay should be banned* from the market.

8. An artist was hired to _____ a book on the birds of this vicinity.*

9. If you _____ on shouting, I shall be compelled* to leave.

10. It would be a disaster* for freedom of the press if the _____ were permitted to tell us what we can read.

11.  James has just about exhausted* his father's patience with his _____ behavior.
12.  Only a brutal* person would _____ someone who is disabled.

---

**Which Word Means.** From the list of 12 new words that follows, choose the one that corresponds to each definition below.

| | | | |
|---|---|---|---|
| outlaw | promote | undernourished | juvenile |
| illustrate | disclose | excessive | bait |
| disaster | censor | culprit | insist |

1.   something used to attract or lure _____
2.   to raise in rank or importance; help to organize _____
3.   a person guilty of a fault or crime _____
4.   to keep firmly to some demand or position _____
5.   to declare unlawful _____
6.   a young person _____
7.   a person who tells others how they should behave _____
8.   to uncover; make known _____
9.   too much; too great; extreme _____
10.  an event that causes much suffering or loss _____
11.  make clear or explain by stories, examples, or other means _____
12.  not sufficiently fed _____

---

**Spotlight on:**    **disaster** — Shakespeare tells us that Romeo and Juliet were star-crossed lovers; that is, they were under the influence of an evil star (*dis-aster*). This belief is not far removed from that of people who follow the horoscopes and those who are concerned about the sign of the zodiac they were born under.

---

**Which of the words studied in this lesson is suggested by the picture?**

# Lesson 29

## Words To Learn This Week

toil
blunder
daze
mourn
subside
maim
comprehend
commend
final
exempt
vain
repetition

1. **toil** (toil) hard work; to work hard; move with difficulty
   a. The feeble* old man **toiled** up the hill.
   b. After years of **toil,** scientists disclosed* that they had made progress in controlling the dreaded* disease.
   c. Despite* all his **toil,** Fred never succeeded in reaching his goal.

2. **blunder** (blun′ dər) stupid mistake; to make a stupid mistake; stumble; say clumsily
   a. The exhausted* boy **blundered** through the woods.
   b. Bert's awkward* apology* could not make up for his serious **blunder.**
   c. The general's **blunder** forced his army to a rapid* retreat.

3. **daze** (dāz) confuse
   a. The severity* of the blow **dazed** the fighter and led to his defeat.
   b. When he ventured* out of the house at night, the child was **dazed** by the noise and the lights.
   c. **Dazed** by the flashlight, Maria blundered* down the steps.

4. **mourn** (môrn) grieve; feel or show sorrow for
   a. Sandra did not cease* to **mourn** her lost friend.
   b. The entire city **mourned** for the people lost in the calamity.*
   c. We need not **mourn** over trifles.*

5. **subside** (səb sīd′) sink to a lower level; grow less
   a. After the excessive* rains stopped, the flood waters **subsided.**
   b. The waves **subsided** when the winds ceased* to blow.
   c. Danny's anger **subsided** when the culprit* apologized.*

6. **maim** (mām) cripple; disable; cause to lose an arm, leg, or other part of the body
   a. Auto accidents **maim** many persons each year.
   b. Though he went through an awesome* experience in the crash, Fred was not seriously **maimed.**
   c. Car manufacturers insist* that seat belts can prevent the **maiming** of passengers in the event of a crash.

7. **comprehend** (käm′ pri hend′) understand
   a. If you can use a word correctly, there is a good chance that you **comprehend** it.
   b. You need not be a pauper* to **comprehend** fully what hunger is.
   c. My parents say that they cannot **comprehend** today's music.

8. **commend** (kə mend′) praise; hand over for safekeeping
   a. Everyone **commended** the mayor's thrifty* suggestion.
   b. Florence **commended** the baby to her aunt's care.
   c. The truth is that we all like to be **commended** for good work.

9. **final** (fī′ nal) coming last; deciding
   a. The **final** week of the term is rapidly* approaching.
   b. Jose was commended* for his improvement in the **final** test.
   c. The **final** censor* of our actions is our own conscience.

10. **exempt** (eg zempt′) make free from; freed from
    a. Our school **exempts** bright pupils from final* exams.
    b. School property is **exempt** from most taxes.
    c. Juvenile* offenders are not **exempt** from punishment.

11. **vain** (vān) having too much pride in one's ability, looks, etc.; of no use
    a. Josephine is quite **vain** about her beauty.
    b. To be perfectly frank, I do not see what she has to be **vain** about.

  c. Brian made numerous* **vain** attempts to reach the doctor by telephone.

12.  **repetition** (rep′ ə tish′ ən) act of doing or saying again
  a. The **repetition** of new words in this book will help you to learn them.
  b. Any **repetition** of such unruly* behavior will be punished.
  c. After a **repetition** of his costly mistake, Jerry was fired from his job.

---

**Which of the words studied in this lesson is suggested by the picture?**

---

*Read the following story to see how the new words are used in it.*

### Camp Safety

For years a furniture salesman from Connecticut, Mitch Kurman, has **toiled** ceaselessly* for the passage of a youth summercamp safety bill. Why? Because his son David was drowned when his canoe overturned in the raging* waters of the Penobscot River. The camp counselors leading the trip were inexperienced, had **blundered** into dangerous waters, and had no life jackets for the canoers.

Mr. Kurman was naturally **dazed** by the tragedy.* But rather than merely **mourn** his loss and wait for the painful memory to **subside,** he began a campaign that took him on hundreds of journeys to speak to governors, senators, and congressmen. He had learned that 250,000 children are injured or **maimed** annually* in camp accidents. It was hard for him to **comprehend** why we have laws that outlaw* mistreatment of alligators, coyotes, birds and bobcats, but we have no law to prevent disasters* to children in summer camps.

Wherever he went, Mr. Kurman was **commended** for his efforts, but he received only trifling* support from the lawmakers. One bill requiring people to put on life preservers when they took to the water "died" in the **final** reading. Another such bill **exempted** private ponds and lakes, exactly the waters where most summer camps are located.* Even a bill calling for a survey of camp safety conditions was at first defeated. Mr. Kurman's struggle so far has been in **vain,** but he continues his battle to avoid*a **repetition** of the accident that took his son's life.

**Place one of the new words in each of the blanks below.**

1. There is a tendency* to _____ politicians from keeping campaign promises.
2. A _____ of such a blunder* could be disastrous.*
3. The guide* was compelled* to admit he had _____ far from the intended route.
4. A miserly* person cannot _____ the joy of sharing.
5. Though doctors _____ to cure the undernourished* child, he never regained his full health.
6. Three workers were _____ when the ladder collapsed.*
7. The policeman was _____ for his bravery in capturing the armed outlaw.*
8. The perfect attendance of our class illustrated* the importance of this _____ exam.
9. Friend and foe united* in_____the death of the leader, for she was respected by all.
10. The drowning man's cries were uttered* in _____, because no one was near to hear them.
11. Miguel's fever _____ after he took the medicine.
12. My brother was in such a _____ over the tragedy* that he could hardly respond* to questions.

---

**Matching.** Match the 12 new words in Column I with the definitions in Column II.

| Column I | Column II |
|---|---|
| _____ 1. comprehend | a. grieve |
| _____ 2. repetition | b. hard work |
| _____ 3. exempt | c. sink to a lower level |
| _____ 4. vain | d. coming last |
| _____ 5. commend | e. stupid mistake |
| _____ 6. maim | f. act of doing or saying again |
| _____ 7. toil | g. praise |
| _____ 8. final | h. make free from |
| _____ 9. blunder | i. understand |
| _____ 10. mourn | j. disable; cripple |
| _____ 11. daze | k. confuse |
| _____ 12. subside | l. having too much pride in one's ability, looks, etc. |

---

**Spotlight on:**    **maim**—If you are a reader of fine print, you might notice that auto insurance policies don't use words like *maim* carelessly because this word has a very specific meaning. *Maim* suggests the loss or destruction of an arm or leg or both; to be *maimed* a person would have to suffer permanent injury. Would the insurance company use the word *mutilate*?

---

# Lesson 30

"You cram these words into mine ears against
The stomach of my sense."

Shakespeare, *The Tempest*

**Words To Learn This Week**

depict
mortal
novel
occupant
appoint
quarter
site
quote
verse
morality
roam
attract

1. **depict** (di pikt′) represent by drawing or painting; describe
   a. The artist and the author both tried to **depict** the sunset's beauty.
   b. Mr. Salinger **depicted** the juvenile* character with great accuracy.*
   c. The extent of the disaster* can scarcely* be **depicted** in words.

2. **mortal** (môr′ tl) sure to die sometime; pertaining to man; deadly; pertaining to or causing death
   a. We must live with the knowledge that all living creatures are **mortal.**
   b. His rash* venture* brought him to a **mortal** illness.
   c. The two monarchs* were **mortal** enemies.

3. **novel** (näv′ l) new; strange; a long story with characters and plot
   a. The architect* created a **novel** design which pleased everyone.
   b. The **novel** plan caused some unforeseen* problems.
   c. Robert was commended* by his teacher for the excellent report on the American **novel**, *The Grapes of Wrath.*

4. **occupant** (äk′ yə pənt) person in possession of a house, office, or position
   a. A feeble* old woman was the only **occupant** of the shack.
   b. The will disclosed* that the **occupant** of the estate was penniless.
   c. The **occupant** of the car beckoned* us to follow him.

5. **appoint** (ə point′) decide on; set a time or place; choose for a position; equip or furnish
   a. The library was **appointed** as the best place for the urgent* meeting.
   b. Though Mr. Thompson was **appointed** to a high position, he did not neglect* his old friends.
   c. The occupant* of the well-**appointed** guest room considered* himself quite fortunate.*

6. **quarter** (kwôr′ tər) region; section; (quarters) a place to live; to provide a place to live
   a. The large family was unaccustomed* to such small **quarters.**
   b. Ellen moved to the French **Quarter** of our city.
   c. The city **quartered** the paupers* in an old school.

7. **site** (sīt) position or place (of anything)
   a. The agent insisted* that the house had one of the best **sites** in town.
   b. We were informed by our guide* that a monument would be built on the **site** of the historic battle.
   c. For the **site** of the new school, the committee preferred an urban* location.*

8. **quote** (kwōt) repeat exactly the words of another or a passage from a book; that is, something that is repeated exactly; give the price of; a quotation
   a. She often **quotes** her spouse* to prove a point.
   b. The stockbroker **quoted** gold at a dollar off yesterday's closing price.
   c. Biblical **quotes** offer a unique* opportunity for study.

9. **verse** (vers) a short division of a chapter in the Bible; a single line or a group of lines of poetry
   a. The **verse** from the Bible which my father quoted* most frequently* was, "Love thy neighbor as thyself."
   b. Several **verses** of a religious nature were contained in the document.*
   c. Though it is not always easy to comprehend,* Shakespeare's **verse** has merit* that is worth the toil.*

10. **morality** (mə ral′ ə tē) the right or wrong of an action; virtue; a set of rules or principles of conduct
    a. The editor* spoke on the **morality** of "bugging" the quarters* of a political opponent.*
    b. We rarely consider* the **morality** of our daily actions though that should occupy* a high position in our thinking.
    c. Kenny's unruly* behavior has nothing to do with his lack* of **morality.**

11. **roam** (rōm) wander; go about with no special plan or aim
    a. In the days of the wild West, outlaws* **roamed** the country.
    b. A variety* of animals once **roamed** our land.
    c. The bachelor* promised his girlfriend that he would **roam** no more.

12. **attract** (a trakt′) draw to oneself; win the attention and liking of
    a. The magnet **attracted** the iron particles.
    b. Adventure was the thrill which **attracted** the famous mountain climber to the jagged* peak.
    c. A glimpse* into the brightly colored room **attracted** the children's attention.

---

*Read the following story to see how the new words are used in it.*

**Bible Zoo**

One of the most popular* tales of the Bible **depicts** the great flood that destroyed every **mortal** except Noah and his family and the animals on his ark. Should there be a repetition* of that disaster,* there is one place where all the biblical animals are already gathered. The man to be commended* for this **novel** collection is Professor Aharon Shulov, a zoologist at Hebrew University in Jerusalem, Israel.

Professor Shulov **appointed** himself a committee of one to search out the 130 creatures mentioned in the Old Testament. Among the **occupants** of this zoo are the crocodiles, camels, apes, peacocks, deer, foxes, and sheep, some of whom had to be imported from other lands. They are settled in suitable **quarters** on a twenty-five acre **site** in Jerusalem.

Visitors to the zoo not only get to view and feed the animals, but they are also treated to **quotes** from Bible **verses** that encourage* the study of the Good Book and teach **morality** amidst the waddling of the ducks and the wailing* of the wolves. Not surprisingly, the children have the final* word at a special corner of the zoo, called the Garden of Eden, where animal cubs **roam** freely, **attracting** the attention of hundreds of youngsters who visit daily.

---

**Place one of the new words in each of the blanks below.**

1. The judge_____to this case must be a person of justice* and honesty.
2. I knew that the culprit* was in _____ terror of being caught.
3. The _____ of the collapsed* building were dazed* by the tragedy.*
4. How can you _____ in a favorable light a person who betrayed* his country?
5. Let us explore* another _____ for the hospital where the population* is not so dense.*
6. A good line of _____ is thrifty* with words and bursting with feeling.
7. Troops were _____ in the city in a vain* attempt to keep order.
8. The price he _____ for the car was essentially* the same as that of his competitor.*
9. Seeing the movie based on the _____ does not exempt* you from reading the book.
10. The death of the millionaire _____ a bewildering* number* of hopeful beneficiaries.*
11. The new _____ has not won unanimous* acceptance; there are those who prefer the traditional* ways.
12. When I _____ abroad,* I come across many historic sites* and structures.

**Exercise**

*Now make up your own sentences, one for each of the new words you have just been taught.*

1. _____
2. _____
3. _____
4. _____
5. _____
6. _____
7. _____
8. _____
9. _____
10. _____
11. _____
12. _____

**Spotlight on:** **mortal**—The main part of this word, *mort-*, comes from the Latin and means "to die." Some words you have heard contain this same root—*mortgage*, *mortify* and *mortuary*. How are they related to the meaning "to die"? In detective stories, watch for the words "rigor mortis."

**Which of the words studied in this lesson is suggested by the picture?**

# Word Review #5

These exercises are based on some of the words which you found in Lessons 25–30.

**A.** In each of the parentheses below there are two choices. Pick the one that fits better.
1. Will storekeepers be (prosecuted, pacified) for raising prices without government permission?
2. With a few strokes of his brush, Norman Rockwell could (depict, commend) beautiful scenes.
3. Eric's serious (toil, blunder) caused him to lose the card game.
4. It is useless to (mourn, maim) over spilt milk.
5. Through his love of racing cars, Trevor (squandered, subsided) all the money he had inherited.
6. Although she was very unhappy, Dora refused to (utter, comprehend) one word of complaint.
7. At each step of the way, signs have been placed to (guide, attract) you through the winding caves.
8. The bachelor* met a lovely girl and decided to enter into (matrimony, bigamy).
9. Willie Mays had a (mortal, novel) way of catching a fly ball which most fans had never seen.
10. I tried to (unite, disrupt) the angry cousins but they would not let me make peace between them.

**B. Opposites.** In Column I are ten words from Lessons 25–30. Match them correctly with their *opposite* meanings in Column II.

| Column I | Column II |
|---|---|
| 1. roam | a. well-fed |
| 2. undernourished | b. strong |
| 3. disclose | c. start |
| 4. rapid | d. could not happen |
| 5. pauper | e. not enough |
| 6. possible | f. stay at home |
| 7. feeble | g. careful |
| 8. cease | h. rich person |
| 9. excessive | i. hide |
| 10. rash | j. slow |

**C.** Which of the vocabulary choices in parentheses fits best in these newspaper headlines?
1. **Flood Waters _____ As Emergency Ends**    (Collapse, Subside, Quench, Respond)
2. **12-Year-Old Mugger Protected By _____ Law**    (Final, Rash, Juvenile, Fugitive)
3. **Diplomat Sent To _____ Angry Canadians**    (Pacify, Prosecute, Betray, Disrupt)
4. **Hundreds At Church _____ For Accident Victims**    (Beckon, Mourn, Respond, Venture)
5. **_____ Fire Expected In Lebanese War**    (Cease, Squander, Compel, Commend)
6. **Former _____ Does Not Miss Royal Luxury**    (Guide, Monarch, Architect, Censor)
7. **Merger Effort Will _____ The Two Companies**    (Daze, Betray, Depict, Unite)
8. **Painter Aims To _____ Life In Haiti**    (Outlaw, Depict, Exhaust, Utter)
9. **Bank Rewards _____ Depositors**    (Rash, Pauper, Excessive, Thrifty)
10. **"Forgetful" Husband Accused Of _____**    (Morality, Bigamy, Toil, Severity)

**D.** From the list of words below choose the word that means:
1. subject to death *and* has the same root as *mortgage*
2. lose a bodily part *and therefore* be crippled or disabled
3. a great misfortune *and* suggests one is under the influence of "an unlucky star"
4. economical or stingy *but also* could describe someone who is prosperous because of hard work and good management
5. one who draws plans for a house *but also* refers to the creator of any plan or idea
6. a person with two wives or two husbands *and* is derived from the Greek word for "two weddings"
7. put out, as a fire, *and also* satisfy, as one's thirst
8. a ruler, rare in modern times *and also* master
9. an official with the power to remove objectionable material from a book or film *as well as* a person who reads mail in wartime, to remove information that might be useful to the enemy
10. provide lodgings *as well as* a particular district or section

| | | | | | |
|---|---|---|---|---|---|
| occupant | disrupt | calamity | morality | utter | pacify |
| site | venture | beckon | toil | subside | commend |
| promote | verse | mortal | culprit | commend | fugitive |
| quench | exempt | maim | compel | architect | monarch |
| censor | quarter | awesome | bigamist | thrifty | disaster |

# Lesson 31

"All my best is dressing old words new."

Shakespeare, *Sonnet lxxvi*

1. **commuter** (kə mūt′ ər) one who travels regularly, especially over a considerable distance, between home and work
   a. The average **commuter** would welcome a chance to live in the vicinity* of his or her work.
   b. Have your **commuter's** ticket verified* by the conductor.
   c. A novel* educational program gives college credit to **commuters** who listen to a lecture while they are traveling to work.

2. **confine** (kən fīn′) keep in; hold in
   a. The fugitive* was caught and **confined** to jail for another two years.
   b. A virus that was circulating* in the area **confined** Al to his house.
   c. Polio **confined** President Roosevelt to a wheelchair.

3. **idle** (ī′ dl) not doing anything; not busy; lazy; without any good reason or cause; to waste (time)
   a. Any attempt to study was abandoned* by the student, who **idled** away the morning.
   b. The **idle** hours of a holiday frequently* provide the best time to take stock.
   c. Do not deceive* yourself into thinking that these are just **idle** rumors.

4. **idol** (ī′ dl) a thing, usually an image, that is worshipped; a person or thing that is loved very much
   a. This small metal **idol** illustrates* the art of ancient Rome.
   b. John Wayne was the **idol** of many young people who liked cowboy movies.
   c. Scientists are still trying to identify* this **idol** found in the ruins.

5. **jest** (jest) joke; fun; mockery; thing to be laughed at; to joke; poke fun
   a. Though he spoke in **jest,** Mark was undoubtedly* giving us a message.
   b. Do not **jest** about matters of morality.*
   c. In some quarters,* honesty and hard work have become subjects of **jest.**

6. **patriotic** (pā trī ät′ ik) loving one's country; showing love and loyal support for one's country
   a. It is **patriotic** to accept your responsibilities to your country.
   b. The **patriotic** attitude of the captive* led him to refuse to cooperate with the enemy.
   c. Nathan Hale's **patriotic** statement has often been quoted:* "I regret that I have but one life to give for my country."

7. **dispute** (dis pūt′) disagree; oppose; try to win; a debate or disagreement
   a. Our patriotic* soldiers **disputed** every inch of ground during the battle.
   b. The losing team **disputed** the contest up until the final* minute of play.
   c. Many occupants* of the building were attracted* by the noisy **dispute.**

8. **valor** (val′ ər) bravery; courage
   a. The **valor** of the Vietnam veterans deserves the highest commendation.*
   b. No one will dispute* the **valor** of Washington's men at Valley Forge.
   c. The fireman's **valor** in rushing into the flaming house saved the occupants* from a horrid* fate.

9. **lunatic** (l oo′ nə tik) crazy person; insane; extremely foolish
   a. Only a **lunatic** would willingly descend* into the monster's cave.
   b. Certain **lunatic** ideas persist* even though they have been rejected* by all logical* minds.
   c. My roommate has some **lunatic** ideas about changing the world.

10. **vein** (vān) mood; a blood vessel that carries blood to the heart; a crack or seam in a rock filled with a different mineral
  a. A **vein** of lunacy* seemed to run in the family.
  b. Mario's wrist was severely* cut by the rock, causing his **vein** to bleed heavily.
  c. Explorations disclosed* the rich **vein** of copper in the mountain.

11. **uneventful** (un' i vent' fəl) without important or striking happenings
  a. After the variety* of bewildering* experiences at the start of our trip, we were happy that the rest of the journey was **uneventful.**
  b. Our annual* class outing proved quite **uneventful.**
  c. The meeting seemed **uneventful** but expert observers realized that important decisions were being made.

12. **fertile** (fir' tl) bearing seeds or fruit; producing much of anything
  a. Chicks hatch from **fertile** eggs.
  b. The loss of their **fertile** lands threw the farmers into a panic.*
  c. A **fertile** mind need never be uneasy* about finding life uneventful.*

---

Read the following story to see how the new words are used in it.

**Record Holders**

*The Guinness Book of World Records* is full of fascinating facts. For example, the champion **commuter** is Bruno Leuthardt of West Germany, who traveled 370 miles each day for ten years to his teaching job and was late only once because of a flood. The record for being buried alive is held by Emma Smith of Ravenshead, England. She was **confined** in a coffin for 100 days. What a way to spend the **idle** hours! Peter Clark of London collected 1276 autographed pictures of famous men and women. Obviously* not all were his **idols** , but he did set a record.

What drives people to these unusual practices? Some are simply done in **jest,** some for **patriotic** reasons. Certainly no one would **dispute** the **valor** of the "record-makers," even if the records themselves may be no more lasting than a popular* song. While one need not be a **lunatic,** he must have a **vein** of recklessness* to participate in such activities as barrel-jumping, high diving, or parachute jumping.

If you are tired of leading a dull, **uneventful** life, remember the mortals* whose **fertile** imaginations have found novel* ways to add excitement to their lives.

---

**Place one of the new words in each of the blanks below.**

1. Celia was left _____ after working so hard all her life.
2. I would _____ that claim if I did not know you were jesting.*
3. This site* will attract many home buyers because of the advantages for the _____.
4. The early pioneers exhibited* great _____ in braving the hardships* of the new frontiers.
5. A _____ of caution* helped Mr. Samler to avoid* the obvious* risks in his new job.
6. It is no misfortune* to spend a few _____ days without excitement and conflict.*
7. The _____ element of society ignores* the warnings about the dangers of drugs.
8. Since the statement was made in _____, it is not a valid* point to argue.
9. I asked my opponent* in the debate* to _____ his remarks to the subject under discussion.
10. How can we transmit* a healthy _____ view to the next generation?
11. Men have always wanted to inhabit* the land where the soil is most _____.
12. People still worship the _____ of greed* and power.

---

**Exercise**
Now make up your own sentences, one for each of the new words you have just been taught.

1. _____

2. _____

3. _____

4. _____

5. _____

6. _____

7. _____

8. _____

9. _____

10. _____

11. _____

12. _____

**Which of the words studied in this lesson is suggested by the picture?**

**Spotlight on:**    **lunatic**—Here's an old word for an old idea; the Romans believed that our minds are affected by the moon — *luna* means "moon" in Latin —and that *lunatics* grew more crazy as the moon became fuller. In primitive civilizations, fear of the full moon was not unusual.

# Lesson 32

**Words To Learn
This Week**

refer
distress
diminish
maximum
flee
vulnerable
signify
mythology
provide
colleague
torment
loyalty

1.  **refer** (ri fir′) hand over; send, direct, or turn for information, help, or action; (refer to) direct attention to or speak about; assign to or think of as caused by
    a.  Let us **refer** the dispute* to the dean.
    b.  Our teacher **referred** us to the dictionary for the meanings of the difficult words in the novel.*
    c.  The speaker **referred** to a verse in the Bible to support his theory.*

2.  **distress** (dis tres′) great pain or sorrow; misfortune; dangerous or difficult situation; to cause pain or make unhappy
    a.  The family was in great **distress** over the accident that maimed* Kenny.
    b.  My teacher was **distressed** by the dismal performance of our class on the final* examination.
    c.  Long, unscheduled delays at the station cause **distress** to commuters.*

3.  **diminish** (də min′ ish) make or become smaller in size, amount or importance
    a.  The excessive* heat **diminished** as the sun went down.
    b.  Our **diminishing** supply of food was carefully wrapped and placed with the baggage.*
    c.  The latest news from the battlefront confirms* the report of **diminishing** military activity.

4.  **maximum** (mak′ sə məm) greatest amount; greatest possible
    a.  Chris acknowledged* that the **maximum** he had ever walked in one day was fifteen miles.
    b.  We would like to exhibit* this rare* collection to the **maximum** number of visitors.
    c.  The committee anticipated* the **maximum** attendance of the first day of the performance.

5.  **flee** (flē) run away; go quickly
    a.  The **fleeing** outlaws* were pursued* by the police.
    b.  One could clearly see the clouds **fleeing** before the wind.
    c.  The majority* of students understand that they cannot **flee** from their responsibilities.

6.  **vulnerable** (vul′ ner ə bl) capable of being injured; open to attack, sensitive to criticism, influences, etc.
    a.  Achilles was **vulnerable** only in his heel.
    b.  The investigator's nimble* mind quickly located the **vulnerable** spot in the defendant's alibi.
    c.  A **vulnerable** target for thieves is a solitary* traveler.

7.  **signify** (sig′ nə fī) mean; be a sign of; make known by signs, words or actions; have importance
    a.  "Oh!" **signifies** surprise.
    b.  A gift of such value **signifies** more than a casual* relationship.
    c.  The word "fragile"* stamped on a carton **signifies** that it must be handled with caution.*

8.  **mythology** (mi thäl′ e jē) legends or stories that usually attempt to explain something in nature
    a.  The story of Proserpina and Ceres explaining the seasons is typical* of Greek **mythology.**
    b.  From a study of **mythology** we can conclude* that the ancients were concerned with the wonders of nature.

    c. Ancient **mythology** survives* to this day in popular* expressions such as "Herculean task" or "Apollo Project."

9. **colleague** (käl′ ēg) associate; fellow worker
    a. The captain gave credit for the victory to his valiant* **colleagues.**
    b. Who would have predicted* that our pedestrian* **colleague** would one day win the Nobel Prize for Medicine?
    c. We must rescue our **colleagues** from their wretched* condition.

10. **torment** (tôr ment′ or tôr′ ment) cause very great pain to; worry or annoy very much; cause of very great pain; very great pain
    a. Persistent* headaches **tormented** him.
    b. The illustrations* in our history text show the **torments** suffered by the victims of the French Revolution.
    c. The logical* way to end the **torment** of doubt over the examination is to spend adequate* time in study.

11. **provide** (pro vīd) to supply; to state as a condition; to prepare for or against some situation
    a. How can we **provide** job opportunities for all our graduates?
    b. Hal said he would bring the ball **provided** he would be allowed to pitch.
    c. The government is obligated, among other things, to **provide** for the common welfare and secure the blessings of peace for all citizens.

12. **loyalty** (loi′ əl tē) faithfulness to a person, government, idea, custom, or the like
    a. The monarch* referred* to his knights' **loyalty** with pride.
    b. Nothing is so important to transmit* to the youth as the sacredness* of **loyalty** to one's country.
    c. Out of a sense of **loyalty** to his friends, Michael was willing to suffer torments,* and he, therefore, refused to identify* his colleagues* in the plot.

*Read the following story to see how the new words are used in it.*

## How Our Language Grows

Many popular* expressions in our language have interesting backgrounds. When we **refer** to a person's weak spot as his "Achilles heel," we are recalling the story of the mighty Greek hero of the Trojan War, Achilles, a warrior of unusual strength and valor.* The mother of Achilles, in whose veins* flowed the blood of the gods, was warned at his birth that her son would die in battle. In great **distress,** she sought to save her son. In order to **diminish** his chances of being hurt and to give him **maximum** protection* in combat, she dipped the infant in the river Styx. The magic waters touched every part of the child's body except the heel that she held in her hand. Thus it happened many years later that as Achilles started to **flee** from an attack, a poisoned arrow struck him in the heel, the only spot where he was **vulnerable.**

Today, the meaning of "Achilles heel" is not confined* to a weak spot in the body but it also **signifies** a weakness in the character of an individual, or in the defenses of a nation, or in the structure of a system.

American politics, rather than **mythology,** provides the explanation for the word "bunk." This word came into the language in 1820 when Felix Walker, the representative from Buncombe County, North Carolina, formed the habit of making long, unnecessary speeches in Congress. When his **colleagues** asked him why he was **tormenting** them so, he **apologized** by saying it was his patriotic* duty to put those speeches in the record out of **loyalty** to his supporters at home. The word "Buncombe" was shortened to "bunk" and came to mean any thought that has little or no worth.

## Place one of the new words in each of the blanks below.

1. The uneventful* flow of news was interrupted by a report of a ship in _____.
2. Our temperature for the day dropped from a _____ of 85 degrees to a minimum* of 70 degrees.
3. The dishonest employee* planned to _____ with several thousand dollars of the company's money.
4. It was easy to see that the club members resented* Phil's _____ them with silly questions.
5. Colonel Bishop's deep sense of _____ to his men signifies* an honest and honorable nature.
6. Elizabeth was finally* persuaded* to _____ for her remark and to pledge* to be more careful in the future.
7. What I admire in Marty is that he never abandoned* his _____ in their time of need.

8. Mr. Harris' manipulation* of the bank funds _____ his greed.*
9. Debra had a tendency* to _____ all her questions to the librarian instead of looking them up herself.
10. The registration for this course has _____ to the point where we must consider* eliminating* it from the curriculum.
11. The names of the days of the week are based on the names of the gods and goddesses of Norse _____.
12. The distressing* fact is that we are all _____ to natural disasters.*

---

**Which Word Means.** From the list of 12 new words that follows, choose the one that corresponds to each definition below.

| | | | |
|---|---|---|---|
| refer | distress | diminish | maximum |
| flee | vulnerable | signify | mythology |
| colleague | torment | apologize | loyalty |

1. be a sign of _____
2. run away _____
3. great pain or sorrow _____
4. greatest amount _____
5. direct, send, or turn for information, help, or action _____
6. faithfulness _____
7. associate; fellow worker _____
8. legends or stories _____
9. capable of being injured _____
10. cause very great pain to _____
11. become smaller in size _____
12. express regret _____

---

**Spotlight on:**  **colleague**—You may hear people use this word, but most writers find it difficult to spell. The word follows no rules and the only way to learn it is to memorize it once and for all. On the other hand, you can probably get along quite well with "associate," but that's not easy to spell either.

---

**Which of the words studied in this lesson is suggested by the picture?**

# Lesson 33

*"I understand a fury in your words,*
*But not the words."*

Shakespeare, *Othello*

1. **volunteer** (väl ən tēr′) person who enters any service of his or her own free will; to offer one's services
   a. The draft has been abolished* and replaced by a **volunteer** army.
   b. Terry did not hesitate* to **volunteer** for the most difficult jobs.
   c. The boys were reluctant* to **volunteer** their services to help clean up after the dance.

2. **prejudice** (prej′ ə dis) an opinion formed without taking time and care to judge fairly; to harm or injure
   a. **Prejudice** against minority* groups will linger* on as long as people ignore* the facts.
   b. Eliminating* **prejudice** should be among the first concerns of a democracy.
   c. The witness's weird* behavior **prejudiced** Nancy's case.

3. **shrill** (shril) having a high pitch; high and sharp in sound; piercing
   a. Despite* their small size, crickets make very **shrill** noises.
   b. The **shrill** whistle of the policeman was warning enough for the fugitive* to stop in his tracks.
   c. A **shrill** torrent* of insults poured from the mouth of the shrieking* woman.

4. **jolly** (jäl′ ē) merry; full of fun
   a. The **jolly** old man, an admitted bigamist,* had forgotten to mention his first wife to his new spouse.*
   b. When the **jolly** laughter subsided,* the pirates began the serious business of dividing the gold.
   c. Are you aware* that a red-suited gentleman with a **jolly** twinkle in his eyes is stuck in the chimney?

5. **witty** (wit′ ē) cleverly amusing
   a. Mr. Carlson's **witty** introduction qualifies* him as a first-rate speaker.
   b. Fay is too slow to appreciate such **witty** remarks.
   c. The lawyer tried to prosecute* the case by being **witty** and thereby entertaining the jury.

6. **hinder** (hin′ dər) hold back; make hard to do
   a. Deep mud **hindered** travel in urban* centers.
   b. The storm **hindered** the pursuit* of the fleeing* prisoners.
   c. Mona's gloomy* nature **hinders** her relationships with other people.

7. **lecture** (lek′ chər) speech or planned talk; a scolding; to scold
   a. Rarely* have I heard a **lecture** with such clear illustrations.*
   b. Henry's father **lectured** him on the awesome* perils* of drug addiction.*
   c. A famous journalist* delivered a **lecture** on prejudice* in the press.

8. **abuse** (ə būz′ or ə būs′) make bad use of; use wrongly; treat badly; scold very severely; bad or wrong use; bad treatment
   a. Those who **abuse** the privileges of the honor system will be penalized.*
   b. The editor* apologized* for the **abuse** we had suffered as a result of his article.
   c. Brutal* **abuse** of children in the orphanage was disclosed* by the investigation.

9. **mumble** (mum′ bl) speak indistinctly
   a. Ricky **mumbled** his awkward* apology.*
   b. This speech course will encourage* you to stop **mumbling** and to speak more distinctly.
   c. When the witness continued to **mumble,** the judge asked him to speak up.

10. **mute** (mūt) silent; unable to speak
    a. The usually defiant* child stood **mute** before the principal.
    b. People are no longer willing to remain **mute** on the subject of abuse* of gun control.
    c. The horror of the famine* left the inhabitants* of the land **mute** with their tragic* memories.

11. **wad** (wăd) small, soft mass; to roll or crush into a small mass
    a. To decrease* the effects of the pressure, the diver put **wads** of cotton in his ears.
    b. The officer challenged* George to explain the **wad** of fifty dollars which he had in his pocket.
    c. Because the automatic firing mechanism was defective,* the hunter had to **wad** the powder into the gun by hand.

12. **retain** (ri tān′) keep; remember; employ by payment of a fee
    a. Despite* her lack* of funds Mrs. Reilly **retained** a detective* to follow her spouse.*
    b. China dishes have the unique* quality* of **retaining** heat longer than metal pans.
    c. Like the majority* of people, I can **retain** the tune but not the words of a song.

---

*Read the following story to see how the new words are used in it.*

### Don't Look over My Shoulder!

The kibitzer is a person who **volunteers** useless information, especially in card games, causing the players to be **prejudiced** against him. The name comes from a Yiddish word which originally referred* to a certain bird whose **shrill** cry scared the animals away upon the approach* of the hunters. Though the kibitzer may think he is being **jolly** or **witty,** his advice often **hinders** more than it helps. We may scowl* at him or **lecture** him for his **abuse** of our friendship, but he still continues to **mumble** his unwelcome remarks. The serious player may even wish he could make the kibitzer **mute** by sticking a **wad** of cotton in his mouth. The kibitzer, however, may not realize that he is causing torment* or distress* to his colleagues.* Thus we may have to resign* ourselves to his annoying habit if we wish to **retain** him as a friend.

---

**Which of the words studied in this lesson is suggested by the picture?**

**Place one of the new words in each of the blanks below.**

1. The culprit* _____ his oath* in court as if his tongue were numb.*
2. The _____ of material stuffed under Mr. Marlowe's shirt made him look bulky* enough to play the part of Santa.
3. With the evidence* mounting* against him, Dr. Parkman was persuaded* to _____ the best lawyer in the state.
4. In a fine showing of loyalty,* many _____ responded* to the fire.
5. Our party was a _____ blend* of good fellowship, song, and dance.
6. The defense attorney made a desperate plea* to the jury not to allow the hazy* evidence* to _____ them against his client.*
7. Edith's fierce* loyalty* has _____ the investigation of the crime.
8. Flynn was usually talkative but the accident left him _____.
9. There were visible* signs that the child had been severely* _____.
10. The _____ screams of the jet planes lead many people to envy* the quiet country life.
11. Father gave Steve a _____ for neglecting* to wash the car.
12. A _____ line in Shakespeare's plays may not get a chuckle in our century.*

---

**Exercise**

*Now make up your own sentences, one for each of the new words you have just been taught.*

1. _____
2. _____
3. _____
4. _____
5. _____
6. _____
7. _____
8. _____
9. _____
10. _____
11. _____
12. _____

---

**Spotlight on:** **prejudice**—Even a newcomer to this word might be able to figure out its meaning from the parts of the word itself; *pre* means "before" and *judge* means "decide." So a person who "decides before" thinking out a problem is *prejudiced*.

# Lesson 34

"His words are a very fantastical banquet, just so many strange dishes."

Shakespeare, *Much Ado About Nothing*

**Words To Learn
This Week**

candidate
precede
adolescent
coeducational
radical
spontaneous
skim
vaccinate
untidy
utensil
sensitive
temperate

1. **candidate** (kan′ də dāt) person who is proposed for some office or honor
   a. We can have a maximum* of four **candidates** for the office of president.
   b. Each **candidate** for mayor seemed confident* he would be victorious.*
   c. The **candidate** took every precaution* to avoid* mentioning his opponent* by name.

2. **precede** (prē sēd′) go before; come before; be higher in rank or importance
   a. Lyndon Johnson **preceded** Richard Nixon as President.
   b. In a gallant* gesture, Ronnie allowed Amanda's name to **precede** his in the program listing.
   c. A prominent* speaker **preceded** the ceremony of the granting of the diplomas.

3. **adolescent** (ad′ ə les′ nt) growing up to manhood or womanhood; youthful; a person from about 13 to 22 years of age
   a. In his **adolescent** years, the candidate* claimed, he had undergone many hardships.*
   b. There is a fiction* abroad* that every **adolescent** is opposed to tradition.*
   c. Our annual* Rock Festival attracts* thousands of **adolescents.**

4. **coeducational** (kō ej′ e ka′ shən l) having to do with educating both sexes in the same school
   a. There has been a massive* shift to **coeducational** schools.
   b. **Coeducational** institutions, once thought to have a disruptive* effect, have been found to be beneficial.*
   c. In choosing a college, Ned leans toward schools which are **coeducational.**

5. **radical** (rad′ ə kl) going to the root; fundamental; extreme; person with extreme opinions
   a. The tendency* to be vicious* and cruel is a **radical** fault.
   b. We observe that the interest in **radical** views is beginning to subside.*
   c. Because Richard was a **radical** the Conservative Party would not accept him as a candidate.*

6. **spontaneous** (spon ta′ nē əs) of one's own free will; natural; on the spur of the moment; without rehearsal
   a. The vast* crowd burst into **spontaneous** cheering at the skillful play.
   b. Be cautious* with these oily rags because they can break out in **spontaneous** flame.
   c. William's **spontaneous** resentment* at the mention of his sister was noted by the observant* teacher.

7. **skim** (skim) remove from the top; move lightly (over); glide along; read hastily or carelessly
   a. This soup will be more nourishing* if you do not **skim** off the fat.
   b. I caught a glimpse* of Mark and Marge **skimming** over the ice.
   c. Detective Corby, assigned to the homicide,* was **skimming** through the victim's book of addresses.

8. **vaccinate** (vak′ sə nāt) inoculate with vaccine as a protection against smallpox and other diseases
   a. There has been a radical* decline in polio since doctors began to **vaccinate** children with the Salk vaccine.
   b. The general population* has accepted the need to **vaccinate** children against the once-dreaded* disease.
   c. Numerous* examples persist* of people who have neglected* to have their infants **vaccinated.**

9. **untidy** (un tī′ dē) not neat; not in order
   a. The bachelor's* quarters* were most **untidy.**
   b. We must start a clean-up campaign to keep the campus* from being so **untidy.**
   c. Finding the house in such an **untidy** condition baffled* us.

10. **utensil** (ū ten′ səl) container or tool used for practical purposes
    a. Several **utensils** were untidily* tossed about the kitchen.
    b. Edward's baggage* contained all the **utensils** he would need on the camping trip.
    c. Some people are so old-fashioned that they reject* the use of any modern **utensil.**

11. **sensitive** (sen′ sə tiv) receiving impressions readily; easily affected or influenced; easily hurt or offended
    a. The eye is **sensitive** to light.
    b. From the experiment we may conclude* that mercury in a thermometer is **sensitive** to changes in temperature.
    c. James is **sensitive** about his wretched* handwriting.

12. **temperate** (tem′ pər it) not very hot and not very cold; moderate
    a. The United States is mostly in the North **Temperate** Zone
    b. All students received the appeal* to be **temperate** and not to jump to conclusions* in judging the new grading system.
    c. Mrs. Rollins commended* her class for their **temperate** attitude when she announced the extra assignment.

---

*Read the following story to see how the new words are used in it.*

## A Course for Parents

A course entitled "The Responsibilities of Parenthood" sounds as if it should be offered to students who are immediate **candidates** for parenthood. Not according to Dr. Lee Salk, who feels that teaching children about parenthood should **precede** the **adolescent** years. Dr. Salk, of the New York Hospital, teaches a volunteer* **coeducational** class of junior high school youngsters what it means to be a parent. He does not lecture* or present **radical** views. Rather, he conducts **spontaneous** discussions by encouraging* students to imagine that they are parents and asking them such questions as "What would you do if you found your child smoking?" or "How would you prepare your child for the first day of school?" The lessons **skim** over such topics as the need

to **vaccinate** children against diseases or to teach them not to be **untidy** or to use **utensils** properly. The class is more concerned with preparing students emotionally to become better parents some day and with making children **sensitive** to the responsibilities of parenthood.

The class members often express **temperate** and mature views. One girl said she would not approve of having a nurse bring up her child. Another felt that money earned through baby-sitting or other jobs should be shared with parents. When asked how his students rate, Dr. Salk retained* a hopeful outlook. "They are ready for this information," he declared. "I think they'll be honest parents."

---

## Place one of the new words in each of the blanks below.

1. It is to Mitchell's credit that he gained a harvest* of friends in his _____ years.
2. The _____ who gets the job must have an adequate* knowledge* of journalism.*
3. Detective Wayne threatened* to take _____ action if the outlaws* did not surrender.
4. You can scarcely* call Jay's hour-long acceptance speech a _____ response* to his victory.
5. If you consent* to have yourself _____ against the Asiatic flu, you will be relieved* of further tension or worry.
6. Brad identified* the_____as a miniature* radiation gauge.
7. Kim is _____ about her poor grades, yet she rejects* offers of help.
8. The warden* tried to soothe* the violent* men by speaking to them in a _____ manner.
9. From the piles of rubbish it is obvious* that the occupant* of this room was an _____ person.
10. The data* show that _____ classes tend to encourage* greater competition* in learning.

11.   A rise in the wholesale* prices _____ the sharp increase on the retail level.
12.   In the hazy* sunlight, we watched the swallows _____ over the water.

---

**Matching.** Match the 12 new words in Column I with the definitions in Column II.

| Column I | Column II |
|---|---|
| _____ 1. sensitive | a.  not very hot and not very cold |
| _____ 2. coeducational | b.  of one's own free will |
| _____ 3. vaccinate | c.  youthful |
| _____ 4. spontaneous | d.  inoculate |
| _____ 5. untidy | e.  having to do with education of both sexes at the same school |
| _____ 6. precede | f.  remove from the top |
| _____ 7. adolescent | g.  extreme |
| _____ 8. radical | h.  person who is proposed for some office |
| _____ 9. utensil | i.  go before |
| _____ 10. candidate | j.  not neat |
| _____ 11. temperate | k.  receiving impressions readily |
| _____ 12. skim | l.  container or tool used for practical purposes |

---

**Which of the words studied in this lesson is suggested by the picture?**

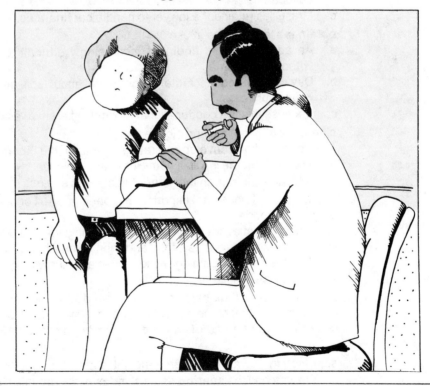

---

**Spotlight on:**   **vaccinate**—The first *vaccines* designed to protect us from disease were discovered by Louis Pasteur in France in 1885. He prepared a serum from cows  ( *vache*  is the word for cow in French) and injected it into his patients. These patients did not contract smallpox, a dreaded disease that was conquered with the first *vaccine*.

# Lesson 35

<table>
<tr><td>

**Words To Learn This Week**

vague
elevate
lottery
finance
obtain
cinema
event
discard
soar
subsequent
relate
stationary

</td></tr>
</table>

1. **vague** (vāg) not definite; not clear; not distinct
   a. Joe's position was **vague** because he wanted to remain neutral* in the dispute.*
   b. When asked her opinion, Gladys was tactful* enough to give a **vague** answer that did not hurt anyone.
   c. The **vague** shape in the distance proved to be nothing more weird* than a group of trees.

2. **elevate** (el′ ə vāt) raise; lift up
   a. Private Carbo was **elevated** to higher rank for his valor.*
   b. Reading a variety* of good books **elevates** the mind.
   c. The candidate* spoke from an **elevated** platform.

3. **lottery** (lot′ ər ē) a scheme for distributing prizes by lot or chance
   a. The merit* of a **lottery** is that everyone has an equal chance.
   b. We thought that a **lottery** was an absurd* way of deciding who should be the team captain.
   c. The rash* young man claimed the **lottery** prize only to find he had misread his number.

4. **finance** (fə nans′) money matters; to provide money for
   a. The new employee* boasted of his skill in **finance.**
   b. Frank circulated* the rumor that his uncle would **finance** his way through college.
   c. Mrs. Giles retained* a lawyer to handle her **finances.**

5. **obtain** (əb tān′) get; be in use
   a. An adolescent* is finding it increasingly difficult to **obtain** a good job without a diploma.
   b. David **obtained** accurate* information about college from his guidance counselor.
   c. Because this is a coeducational* school, different rules **obtain** here.

6. **cinema** (sin′ ə mə) moving picture
   a. Censors* have developed a rating system for the **cinema.**
   b. Today's **cinema** is full of homicides* and violence.*
   c. A best-seller is often the source* of **cinema** stories.

7. **event** (i vent′) happening; important happening; result or outcome; one item in a program of sports
   a. The greatest **event** in Ellie's life was winning the $50,000 lottery.*
   b. We chose our seat carefully and then awaited the shot-put **event.**
   c. There is merit* in gaining wisdom even after the **event.**

8. **discard** (dis kärd′) throw aside
   a. Anna casually* **discarded** one boy friend after another.
   b. Confident* that he held a winning hand, Slim refused to **discard** anything.
   c. Asked why he had **discarded** his family traditions,* Mr. Menzel remained mute.*

9. **soar** (sôr) fly upward or at a great height; aspire
   a. We watched the **soaring** eagle skim* over the mountain peak.
   b. An ordinary man cannot comprehend* such **soaring** ambition.
   c. The senator's hopes for victory **soared** after his television appearance.

10. **subsequent** (sub′ sə kwənt) later; following; coming after
    a. **Subsequent** events* proved that Sloan was right.
    b. Further explanations will be presented in **subsequent** lectures.*

c. Though the enemy forces resisted* at first, they **subsequently** learned that their efforts were in vain.*

11. **relate** (rə lāt′) tell; give an account of; connect in thought or meaning
   a. The traveler **related** his adventures with some exaggeration.*
   b. After viewing the cinema's* latest show, the observant* student was able to **relate** every detail.
   c. Would you say that misfortune* is **related** to carelessness?

12. **stationary** (stā′ shən er′ ē) having a fixed station or place; standing still; not moving; not changing in size, number or activity
   a. A factory engine is **stationary.**
   b. The population* of our town has been **stationary** for a decade.*
   c. Caught in the middle of traffic, the frightened pedestrian* remained **stationary** in the busy street.

---

*Read the following story to see how the new words are used in it.*

### Summer Travel

If you are tired of making **vague** excuses for another dull summer at home, here is a thought to **elevate** your spirits. You do not need anything so radical* as winning a **lottery** to **finance** a trip to Europe. A student identity card that can be **obtained** for a few dollars from the Council on International Educational Exchange entitles you to discount tickets on certain charter flights to London and Paris, as well as reduced admission to many museums, **cinemas,** and musical **events.**

Once in Europe, you can stretch your budget by staying at approved* youth hostels for about two dollars a night. So don't **discard** your hopes of becoming an international traveler. Soon you can be **soaring** into the skies or skimming* over the waves to new adventures that you will **subsequently relate** to your **stationary** friends.

---

**Which of the words studied in this lesson is suggested by the picture?**

**Place one of the new words in each of the blanks below.**

1. Our club consented* to hold a _____ as a means of raising money.
2. If you want to _____ data* on employment opportunities, a good source* is the Bulletin of the Department of Labor.
3. Some call it a _____ but I call it a movie.
4. Our team excelled* in the last _____ of the track meet.
5. As I watched the huge jet _____ into the sky, I wished that I were on board.
6. Since Margaret has become his neighbor, Bud's progress in school has been practically _____.
7. _____ to his phone call, I received a confirmation* in the mail.
8. We are compelled* to _____ this outdated theory.*
9. How does that evidence* _____ to the case?
10. Tim's argument may be logical* but it is too _____ to be convincing.
11. With no one to _____ the project, the entire scheme collapsed.*
12. This feeble* speech will do little to _____ the spirits of the audience.

---

**Which Word Means.** From the list of 12 new words that follows, choose the one that corresponds to each definition below.

| | | | |
|---|---|---|---|
| elevate | obtain | soar | vague |
| relate | stationary | lottery | discard |
| cinema | subsequent | finance | event |

1. raise; lift up _____
2. later; following; coming after _____
3. moving picture _____
4. important happening _____
5. fly upward or at a great height; aspire _____
6. not definite; not clear; not distinct _____
7. not moving _____
8. a scheme for distributing prizes by lot or chance _____
9. tell; connect in thought or meaning _____
10. get; be in use _____
11. money matters; to provide money for _____
12. throw aside _____

---

**Spotlight on:**    **cinema**—French words like *cinema* are common in English, and the French have adopted many of our words as well. Our words *weekend* and *drugstore* are heard every day in France. In our country French words are often used to imply high quality. When you pay five dollars, you go to the *cinema*, not the movies.

---

# Lesson 36

"Here are a few of the unpleasant'st words
That ever blotted paper."

Shakespeare, *The Merchant of Venice*

---

## Words To Learn This Week

prompt
hasty
scorch
tempest
soothe
sympathetic
redeem
resume
harmony
refrain
illegal
narcotic

1. **prompt** (prämpt) quick; on time; done at once; to cause (someone) to do something; remind (someone) of the words or actions needed
   a. Be **prompt** in assembling* your baggage.*
   b. Terry's caution* **prompted** him to ask many questions before he consented.*
   c. Larry was confident* he knew his lines well enough not to need any **prompting.**

2. **hasty** (hās′ tē) quick; hurried; not well thought out
   a. A **hasty** glance* convinced him that he was being followed.
   b. Rather than make a **hasty** decision, Mr. Torres rejected* the offer.
   c. Myra apologized* for the **hasty** visit.

3. **scorch** (skôrch) burn slightly; dry up; criticize sharply
   a. The hot iron **scorched** the tablecloth.
   b. Farmers reported that their wheat was being **scorched** by the fierce* rays of the sun.
   c. Mr. Regan gave the class a **scorching** lecture* on proper behavior in the cafeteria.

4. **tempest** (tem′ pist) violent* storm with much wind; a violent disturbance
   a. The **tempest** drove the ship on the rocks.
   b. Following the weather report of the approaching* **tempest,** we were prompted* to seek immediate shelter.
   c. When Mr. Couche saw that a **tempest** was brewing over the issue, he hastily* called a meeting.

5. **soothe** (sōō th) quiet; calm; comfort
   a. With an embrace,* the mother **soothed** the hurt child.
   b. Heat **soothes** some aches; cold **soothes** others.
   c. Rosalie's nerves were **soothed** by the soft music.

6. **sympathetic** (sim′ pə thet′ ik) having or showing kind feelings toward others; approving; enjoying the same things and getting along well together
   a. Judge Cruz was **sympathetic** to the lawyer's plea* for mercy.
   b. Father was fortunately* **sympathetic** to my request to use the car on weekends.
   c. We were all **sympathetic** to Suzanne over her recent* misfortune.*

7. **redeem** (ri dēm′) buy back; pay off; carry out; set free; make up for
   a. The property on which money has been lent is **redeemed** when the loan is paid back.
   b. My family was relieved* to hear that the mortgage had been **redeemed.**
   c. Mr. Franklin promptly* **redeemed** his promise to help us in time of need.

8. **resume** (rə zōōm′) begin again; go on; take again
   a. **Resume** reading where we left off.
   b. Those standing may **resume** their seats.
   c. The violinist **resumed** playing after the intermission.

9. **harmony** (här′ mə nē) situation of getting on well together or going well together; sweet or musical sound
   a. We hoped the incident would not disrupt* the **harmony** that existed between the brothers.
   b. I am sympathetic* to Warren because his plans are in **harmony** with mine.
   c. We responded* to the **harmony** of the song by humming along.

10.  **refrain** (ri frān') hold back
     a.  **Refrain** from making hasty* promises.
     b.  Milo could not **refrain** from laughing at the jest.*
     c.  If you want to be heard, you must **refrain** from mumbling.*

11.  **illegal** (i lē' gl) not lawful; against the law
     a.  It is **illegal** to reveal* the names of juvenile* delinquents.*
     b.  Bigamy* is **illegal** in the United States.
     c.  Mr. Worthington's **illegal** stock manipulations* led to his jail sentence.

12.  **narcotic** (när kät' ik) drug that produces drowsiness, sleep, dullness, or an insensible condition, and lessens pain by dulling the nerves
     a.  Opium is a powerful **narcotic.**
     b.  We do not have adequate* knowledge of the **narcotic** properties of these substances.
     c.  The doctor prescribed a **narcotic** medicine to soothe* the patient's suffering.

---

*Read the following story to see how the new words are used in it.*

**A Helping Hand**

Youth workers Bill Nash and Jim Boyle are house-hunters, not so much for a house as for a concerned family willing to house and feed troubled youngsters temporarily. They try to give **prompt** attention to those who cannot or will not live at home.

For some, leaving home may have been the result of a **hasty** decision, based on a **scorching** remark and the subsequent* **tempest** within the family. The cooling-off period away from the family is a time to **soothe** feelings. With **sympathetic** outsiders, youngsters have a chance to **redeem** themselves. The hope, of course, is that they will learn to relate* to adults again and quickly **resume** a normal life of **harmony** with their own families.

Some people **refrain** from offering their homes, expressing vague* fears of the harmful effects on their own children. But this has not been the case, even when the problem of the "visitor" was the **illegal** use of **narcotics.** One parent remarked, "With us it worked the other way. The horror of drugs became real to my own son. We got a lot more than we gave."

---

**Place one of the new words in each of the blanks below.**

1.  I insist* on a _____ answer to my question.
2.  Harriet's anger was subsequently* _____ by the apology.*
3.  The minister said those who are not _____ from sin will perish.*
4.  Joseph could not _____ from embracing* his long-lost brother.
5.  My cat and dog, though traditionally* enemies, have lived in perfect _____ for years.
6.  Because he liked to be prompt,* Sal ate only a _____ meal.
7.  The farmers were grateful* that the _____ had not destroyed their harvest.*
8.  Jenny picked up the hot iron just as it was about to _____ my shirt.
9.  The couple seemed so _____ that the break-up baffled* us.
10. Chris Pollaro _____ his former position with the company.
11. It is _____ to own firearms without a license.
12. It is impossible* to estimate* the harm caused by the illegal* use of _____.

---

**Exercise**

*Now make up your own sentences, one for each of the new words you have just been taught.*

1.  _____
2.  _____
3.  _____

4. _____

5. _____

6. _____

7. _____

8. _____

9. _____

10. _____

11. _____

12. _____

**Spotlight on:**   **narcotics**—The age of a word can often give us a clue as to the age of the substance it describes. It seems that *narcotics* are indeed ageless. The word itself has been traced back to an ancient language called Indo-European, but we are certain it was used in the Golden Age of Greece. In those times, as now, *narcotics* were used to reduce pain.

**Which of the words studied in this lesson is suggested by the picture?**

# Word Review #6

These exercises are based on some of the words which you found in Lessons 31–36.

**A.** In each of the parentheses below there are two choices. Pick the one that fits better.

1. When he was asked to (relate, confine) his story to the judge, Mr. Parsons grew very nervous.
2. I was surprised to get such a (prompt, shrill) answer to my letter since I had only mailed it on Tuesday.
3. After drinking for three hours, Corky had only a (subsequent, vague) memory of what had taken place at the party.
4. Because my father works in the post office, he can (redeem, obtain) the new stamps which come out each month.
5. Mrs. Sykes stopped her daughter's piano lessons in June but will (resume, refrain) them in September.
6. We could see that the cook was (distressed, soothed) by his wild looks and his violent curses.
7. The cowboys knew that if they lit a fire they would be (vulnerable, temperate) to attack by the outlaws.*
8. Everyone agreed that the Wright brothers' idea about flying was a (radical, sensitive) one.
9. It was an (uneventful, idol) week for us because no one telephoned and no one came to visit.
10. Gina gave (maximum, stationary) attention to her little sister after their mother died.

**B. Opposites.** In Column I are ten words from Lessons 31–36. Match them correctly with their *opposite* meanings in Column II.

| Column I | Column II |
|---|---|
| 1. hasty | a. remain |
| 2. idle | b. lower |
| 3. flee | c. talkative |
| 4. mumble | d. neat |
| 5. jolly | e. sad |
| 6. elevate | f. grow larger |
| 7. discard | g. slow |
| 8. mute | h. keep |
| 9. diminish | i. speak clearly |
| 10. untidy | j. busy |

**C.** Which of the vocabulary choices in parentheses fits best in these newspaper headlines?

1. **Health Department To _____ Kindergartners**    (Diminish, Retain, Vaccinate, Sooth)
2. **Closing Of Factory Causes 450 To Be _____**    (Idol, Temperate, Idle, Sympathetic)
3. **Giants' Chances Are _____ With Loss To Phils**    (Resumed, Elevated, Fertile, Diminished)
4. **Divers To _____ Search For Sunken Vessel**    (Resume, Redeem, Precede, Signify)
5. **Deny _____ Against Older Workers**    (Distress, Prejudice, Dispute, Loyalty)
6. **_____ Professors Speak Out Against Nuclear Plant**    (Illegal, Sympathetic, Radical, Adolescent)
7. **Teenage _____ To Sing In Rock Musical**    (Colleague, Idol, Mute, Jest)
8. **Our Shoreline _____ To Erosion**    (Confined, Related, Vulnerable, Retained)
9. **Frat Members Spend _____ Night In Cemetery**    (Uneventful, Vague, Hasty, Prompt)
10. **_____ Refuses To Pay Until Trains Are Cleaned**    (Colleague, Commuter, Volunteer, Jest)

**D.** From the list of words below choose the word that means:

1. insane *and* is related to the Latin word for "moon"
2. a fellow worker *and* sounds like (and is in fact derived from the same source as) *college*
3. unreasonable opinion *and* indicates a closed mind
4. protect against disease *and* is based on the French word for "cow"
5. a motion picture *and* is the first element of _____tography and _____scope
6. unable to speak *and also* may refer to the softening of colors and tones as well as sounds
7. occurring naturally *and* appears in phrases like "_____ applause" and "_____ generation"
9. reject or throw away *and* would be appropriate in a poker game
10. save from sin *as well as* recover ownership

| | | | | | |
|---|---|---|---|---|---|
| harmony | candidate | subsequent | hinder | diminish | confine |
| soothe | tempest | utensil | abuse | signify | idol |
| radical | soar | temperate | lunatic | Loyalty | vaccinate |
| cinema | mute | shrill | lottery | commuter | discard |
| redeem | spontaneous | prejudice | retain | colleague | fertile |

# Lesson 37

*"Zounds! I was never so bethump'd with words
Since I first call'd my brother's father dad."*

Shakespeare, *King John*

---

1. **heir** (ãr) person who has a right to someone's property after that one dies; person who inherits anything
   a. Though Mr. Sloane is the **heir** to a gold mine, he lives like a miser.*
   b. The monarch* died before he could name an **heir** to the throne.
   c. It is essential* that we locate the rightful **heir** at once.

2. **majestic** (mə jes′ tik) grand; noble; dignified; kingly
   a. The lion is the most **majestic** creature of the jungle.
   b. In Greek mythology,* Mt. Olympus was the **majestic** home of the gods.
   c. The graduates marched into the auditorium to the music of the **majestic** symphony.

3. **dwindle** (dwin′ dl) become smaller and smaller; shrink
   a. Our supply of unpolluted* water has **dwindled.**
   b. With no visible* signs of their ship, hopes for the men's safety **dwindled** with each passing hour.
   c. After the furious tempest,* the **dwindling** chances of finding the raft vanished* entirely.

4. **surplus** (sir′ pləs) amount over and above what is needed; excess, extra
   a. The bank keeps a large **surplus** of money in reserve.
   b. **Surplus** wheat, cotton, and soybeans are shipped abroad.*
   c. No mortal* ever considers* that he has a **surplus** of good things.

5. **traitor** (trā′ ter) person who betrays his or her country, a friend, duty, etc.
   a. The patriot* sneered* when asked to stand on the same platform with the man who was accused of being a **traitor.**
   b. No villain* is worse than a **traitor** who betrays* his country.
   c. Do not call him a **traitor** unless you can verify* the charge.

6. **deliberate** (di lib′ ər āt or di lib′ ər it) to consider carefully; intended; done on purpose; slow and careful, as though allowing time to decide what to do
   a. Rico's excuse was a **deliberate** lie.
   b. My grandfather walks with **deliberate** steps.
   c. Judge Sirica **deliberated** for a week before making his decision known.

7. **vandal** (van′ dl) person who wilfully or ignorantly destroys or damages beautiful things
   a. Adolescent* **vandals** wrecked the cafeteria.
   b. The **vandals** deliberately* ripped the paintings from the wall.
   c. We could scarcely* believe the damage caused by the **vandals.**

8. **drought** (drout) long period of dry weather; lack of rain; lack of water; dryness
   a. Because of the **drought**, some farmers began to migrate* to more fertile* regions.
   b. In time of **drought,** the crops become scorched.*
   c. As the **drought** wore on, people began to grumble against those who had squandered* water when it was more plentiful.

9. **abide** (ə bīd′) accept and follow out; remain faithful to; dwell; endure
   a. The team decided unanimously* to **abide** by the captain's ruling.
   b. Senator Ervin **abided** by his promise not to allow demonstrations in the committee room.
   c. My mother cannot **abide** dirt and vermin.*

10. **unify** (ū′ nə fī) unite; make or form into one
    a. The novel* traces the developments that **unified** the family.
    b. After the Civil War our country became **unified** more strongly.

      c.  It takes a great deal of training to **unify** all these recruits into an efficient fighting machine.

11.  **summit** (sum′ it) highest point; top
    a.  We estimated* the **summit** of the mountain to be twenty thousand feet.
    b.  Do not underestimate* Ruth's ambition to reach the **summit** of the acting profession.
    c.  The **summit** meeting of world leaders diminished* the threat* of war.

12.  **heed** (hēd) give careful attention to; take notice of; careful attention
    a.  I demand that you **heed** what I say.
    b.  Florence pays no **heed** to what the signs say.
    c.  Take **heed** and be on guard against those who try to deceive* you.

**Which of the words studied in this lesson is suggested by the picture?**

*Read the following story to see how the new words are used in it.*

### Listen to Smoky the Bear

At one time the United States was **heir** to great riches, for more than half of our country was covered with forests. Now the **majestic** woodlands have **dwindled** to the point where we have no **surplus** of trees. Of course, only a **traitor** to the beauties of nature would **deliberately** set a forest fire, but careless citizens are the **vandals** who are responsible for much of the destruction. In time of **drought** especially, scorching* fires started by careless smokers can reduce a beautiful forest to acres of blackened stumps.

Theodore Roosevelt understood that we cannot **abide** the continual loss of our precious forests but we must learn to live in harmony* with nature. In 1905 he appointed* Gifford Pinchot to head the Forest Service which promptly* began to **unify** efforts in caring for our national forests. The modern forest rangers, from the "lookouts" stationed on mountain **summits** to the "smokejumpers" who parachute from airplanes to fight fires, ask us to **heed** the advice of Smoky the Bear, who has become their symbol.* Smoky says, "Only *you* can prevent forest fires."

**Place one of the new words in each of the blanks below.**

1. The exhausted* regiment _____ down to a few troops.
2. Secret documents* listed the _____ to the large fortune.
3. Iris made a _____ attempt to ignore* their biting comments.
4. The _____ of waste materials has polluted* our rivers.
5. Charles blundered* off in the wrong direction without _____ my warning cries.
6. Lincoln tried in vain* to keep the North and South _____.
7. It did not take long before the unruly* crowd turned into a mob of howling _____.
8. The confirmed* bachelor* could not _____ having anyone touch a single utensil* in his home.
9. If the _____ does not end soon, I can predict* a famine.*
10. The population* rise will reach its _____ in a few years and then it will level off.
11. Lt. Jenkins lost every morsel* of self-respect and became a _____ to his flag.
12. The loyal* captain, _____ in defeat, won the sympathy* of the people.

---

**Antonyms (opposites).** Circle the word that most nearly expresses the opposite meaning of the word printed in heavy black type.

1. **vandal**
   a. repairer
   b. arsonist
   c. captive*
   d. adolescent*
   e. informer

2. **abide**
   a. discard*
   b. dispute*
   c. deprive*
   d. provide
   e. summon

3. **summit**
   a. tempest*
   b. beneficiary
   c. duplicate*
   d. base
   e. finance*

4. **surplus**
   a. scarceness*
   b. harmony*
   c. hindrance
   d. assistance
   e. rejection

5. **majestic**
   a. fertile*
   b. theatrical
   c. courteous
   d. harsh
   e. ordinary

6. **drought**
   a. ambush*
   b. flood
   c. hardship*
   d. earthquake
   e. windstorm

7. **unify**
   a. separate
   b. redeem*
   c. abuse*
   d. confine*
   e. compress

8. **deliberate**
   a. unintentional
   b. subsequent*
   c. reassuring
   d. comprehensive*
   e. ingenious*

9. **traitor**
   a. addict*
   b. amateur*
   c. bachelor*
   d. patriot*
   e. lunatic*

10. **heed**
    a. abuse*
    b. ignore*
    c. hinder*
    d. discard*
    e. vaccinate*

11. **heir**
    a. evil sinner
    b. accurate reporter
    c. double dealer
    d. fair judge
    e. disinherited son

12. **dwindle**
    a. ignore*
    b. illustrate*
    c. arrest
    d. mumble
    e. increase

---

**Spotlight on:**　**drought**—Yes, the *gh* is silent as in "might" and several other English words. Why? Well, *drought* was an old English word with the *gh* sound pronounced. When the French invaded and conquered England, they brou*gh*t (there it is again) their language and it had no *gh* sound in it. Eventually their influence was so great that English words containing *gh* took on French pronunciation.

# Lesson 38

*"Believe my words
For they are certain and unfallible."*

Shakespeare, I Henry VI

**Words To Learn
This Week**

biography
drench
swarm
wobble
tumult
kneel
dejected
obedient
recede
tyrant
charity
verdict

1. **biography** (bī ăg′ rə fē) the written story of a person's life; the part of literature which consists of biographies
   a. Our teacher recommended* the **biography** of the architect* Frank Lloyd Wright.
   b. The reading of a **biography** gives a knowledge of people and events* that cannot always be obtained* from history books.
   c. The **biography** of Malcolm X is a popular* book in our school.

2. **drench** (drench) wet thoroughly; soak
   a. A heavy rain **drenched** the campus,* and the students had to dry out their wet clothing.
   b. The **drenching** rains resumed* after only one day of sunshine.
   c. His fraternity friends tried to **drench** him but he was too clever for them.

3. **swarm** (swôrm) group of insects flying or moving about together; crowd or great number; to fly or move about in great numbers
   a. As darkness approached,* the **swarms** of children playing in the park dwindled* to a handful.
   b. The mosquitoes **swarmed** out of the swamp.
   c. Our campus* **swarmed** with new students in September.

4. **wobble** (wäb′ l) move unsteadily from side to side
   a. Little Perry thrust* his feet into the oversized shoes and **wobbled** over to the table.
   b. A baby **wobbles** when it begins to walk alone.
   c. Lacking experience on the high wire, the clown **wobbled** along until he reached the safety of the platform.

5. **tumult** (tu′ mŭlt or to͞o′ mult) noise; uproar; violent* disturbance or disorder
   a. The sailors' voices were too feeble* to be heard above the **tumult** of the storm.
   b. There was such a **tumult** in the halls we concluded* an accident had occurred.
   c. The dreaded* cry of "Fire!" caused a **tumult** in the theatre.

6. **kneel** (nēl) go down on one's knees; remain on the knees
   a. Myra **knelt** down to pull a weed from the drenched* flower bed.
   b. The condemned* man **knelt** before the monarch* and pleaded* for mercy.
   c. **Kneeling** over the still figure, the lifeguard tried to revive* him.

7. **dejected** (di jek′ tid) in low spirits; sad
   a. His biography* related* that Edison was not **dejected** by failure.
   b. The defeated candidate* felt **dejected** and scowled* when asked for an interview.
   c. There is no reason to be **dejected** because we did not get any volunteers.*

8. **obedient** (ō bē′ dē ənt) doing what one is told; willing to obey
   a. The **obedient** dog came when his master beckoned.*
   b. **Obedient** to his father's wishes, Guy did not explore* any further.
   c. When parents make reasonable requests of them, the majority* of my friends are **obedient**.

9. **recede** (ri sēd′) go back; move back; slope backward; withdraw
   a. As you ride past in a train, you have the unique* feeling that houses and trees are **receding**.
   b. Mr. Ranford's beard conceals* his **receding** chin.
   c. Always cautious,* Mr. Camhi **receded** from his former opinion.

10. **tyrant** (tī′ rənt) cruel or unjust ruler; cruel master; absolute ruler
    a. Some **tyrants** of Greek cities were mild and fair rulers.
    b. The **tyrant** demanded loyalty* and obedience* from his subjects.
    c. Though Ella was a **tyrant** as director of the play, the whole cast was grateful* to her when the final curtain came down.

11. **charity** (char′ ə tē) generous giving to the poor; institutions for helping the sick, the poor, or the helpless; kindness in judging people's faults
    a. A free hospital is a noble **charity**.
    b. The entire community is the beneficiary* of Henry's **charity**.
    c. The hired hand was too proud to accept help or **charity**.

12. **verdict** (vėr′ dikt) decision of a jury; judgment
    a. The jury returned a **verdict** of guilty for the traitor.*
    b. We were cautioned* not to base our **verdict** on prejudice.*
    c. Baffled* by the **verdict**, the prosecutor* felt that the evidence* had been ignored.*

---

*Read the following story to see how the new words are used in it.*

## Gulliver's Travels

Jonathan Swift tried to show the smallness of people by writing the **biography** of Dr. Lemuel Gulliver. In one of his strangest adventures, Gulliver was shipwrecked. **Drenched** and weary,* he fell asleep on the shore. In the morning, he found himself tied to pegs in the ground, and **swarming** over him were hundreds of little people six inches high.

After a time he was allowed to stand, though he began to **wobble** from being bound so long. He was then marched through the streets, naturally causing a **tumult** wherever he went. Even the palace was not big enough for him to enter, nor could he **kneel** before the king and queen. But he did show his respect for them in another way.

The king was **dejected** because he feared an invasion of Lilliput by Blefuscu, the enemy across the ocean. The reason for the war between the two tiny peoples would seem small and foolish to us. The rebels of Blefuscu were originally Lilliputians who would not abide* by the royal decision to crack their eggs on the small end instead of on the larger end. Gulliver, **obedient** to the king's command, waded out into the water when the tide **receded,** and sticking a little iron hook into each of fifty warships, he pulled the entire enemy fleet to Lilliput. Gulliver later escaped from Lilliput when he realized the tiny king was really a **tyrant** with no **charity** in his heart.

Oddly enough, the **verdict** of generations of readers has taken no heed* of the author's intention in *Gulliver's Travels.* Instead, while Lilliputians are still the symbol* of small, narrow-minded people, Swift's savage attack upon humankind has become one of the best-loved children's classics.

---

**Place one of the new words in each of the blanks below.**

1. The principal probed* the cause of the _____ in the cafeteria.
2. A _____ of insects descended* on the picnic food.
3. When asked for their _____ on the agreement, the members gave their approval spontaneously.*
4. The first project in our creative writing class was a _____ of a close friend or relative.
5. Until the flood waters _____, the authorities prohibited* anyone from returning to the vicinity.*
6. Mr. Finley was redeemed* in the eyes of his employees* by his _____ in overlooking their costly error.
7. The grateful* traveler would _____ in prayer every night.
8. Mother is an expert at soothing* our _____ spirits.
9. It is absurd* to surrender your rights to a _____ when you have abundant* reason to remain free.
10. We faced the dilemma* of being _____ in the downpour while we covered our boat or having to bail the water out of the boat after the rain had ceased.*
11. Melinda shrieked* as the unstable* pedestrian* _____ into the path of the oncoming car.
12. A glance* from the mother was enough of a reminder to bring the _____ child back to her side.

**True or False.** Based on the way the new word is used, write T (true) or F (false) next to the sentence.

_____ 1. A **swarm** is a small group.

_____ 2. To be **obedient** is to do what you are told; to be willing to obey.

_____ 3. A painting of a woman **kneeling** shows the woman walking with a parasol.

_____ 4. A **biography** is the written story of a person's life.

_____ 5. When reporters describe the **tumult** in the streets, they are referring to the noisy mob.

_____ 6. To **recede** is to go forward.

_____ 7. If you get **drenched,** you'll be soaking wet.

_____ 8. The jury's decision is called the **verdict.**

_____ 9. I was **dejected** to learn that I had won the lottery.

_____ 10. A **tyrant** is a just and kind ruler.

_____ 11. To **wobble** is to move unsteadily from side to side.

_____ 12. To show **charity** in judging others is to be kind and lenient in judging their faults.

---

**Spotlight on:**    **biography** — This is a good time to settle an easy question. A _biography_ is a book written about a person's life. The author may write of someone else's life or his or her own; however, when a book is written about one's own life, it's more accurately labeled an _auto_biography.

---

**Which of the words studied in this lesson is suggested by the picture?**

# Lesson 39

"Ah, kill me with thy weapon, not with words!"

Shakespeare, *III Henry VI*

**Words To Learn This Week**

unearth
depart
coincide
cancel
debtor
legible
placard
contagious
clergy
customary
transparent
scald

1. **unearth** (un ėrth′) dig up; discover; find out
   a. The digging of the scientists **unearthed** a buried city.
   b. A plot to defraud* the investors was **unearthed** by the F.B.I.
   c. The museum exhibited* the vase which had been **unearthed** in Greece.

2. **depart** (di pärt′) go away; leave; turn away (from); change; die
   a. We arrived in the village in the morning and **departed** that night.
   b. Stan was vague* about **departing** from his usual manner of choosing a partner.
   c. Vera was reluctant* to mention that her uncle had long since **departed.**

3. **coincide** (kō′ in sid′) occupy the same place in space; occupy the same time; correspond exactly; agree
   a. If these triangles were placed one on top of the other, they would **coincide.**
   b. Because Pete's and Jim's working hours **coincide,** and they live in the same vicinity,* they depart* from their homes at the same time.
   c. My verdict* on the film **coincides** with Adele's.

4. **cancel** (kan′ sl) cross out; mark so that it cannot be used; wipe out; call off
   a. The stamp was only partially* **canceled.**
   b. Because the first shipment contained defective* parts, Mr. Zweben **canceled** the rest of the order.
   c. Having found just the right man for the job, Captain Mellides **canceled** all further interviews.

5. **debtor** (det′ ər) person who owes something to another
   a. If I borrow a dollar from you, I am your **debtor.**
   b. As a **debtor** who had received many favors from the banker, Mr. Mertz was reluctant* to testify against him.
   c. A gloomy* **debtor's** prison was once the fate of those who could not repay their loans.

6. **legible** (lej′ ə bl) able to be read; easy to read; plain and clear
   a. Julia's handwriting is beautiful and **legible.**
   b. Nancy hesitated* in her reading because the words were scarcely* **legible.**
   c. Our teacher penalizes* us for compositions which are not **legible.**

7. **placard** (plak′ ärd) a notice to be posted in a public place; poster
   a. Colorful **placards** announced an urgent* meeting.
   b. **Placards** were placed throughout the neighborhood by rival* groups.
   c. Numerous* **placards** appeared around the city calling for volunteers.*

8. **contagious** (kan tāj′ əs) spreading by contact, easily spreading from one to another
   a. Scarlet fever is **contagious.**
   b. I find that yawning is often **contagious.**
   c. Interest in the project was **contagious,** and soon all opposition to it collapsed.*

9. **clergy** (kler′ jē) persons prepared for religious work; clergymen as a group
   a. We try never to hinder* the **clergy** as they perform their sacred* tasks.
   b. Friar Tuck was a member of the **clergy** who loved a jolly* jest.*
   c. The majority* of the **clergy** felt the new morality* was a menace* to society.

10. **customary** (kus′ təm er′ ē) usual
    a. It was **customary** for wealthy Romans to recline* while they were dining.
    b. The Beatles' movie received the **customary** rave* reviews from the critics.

     c.   The traitor* rejected* the **customary** blindfold for the execution.

11.   **transparent** (trans par′ ənt) easily seen through; clear
     a.   Window glass is **transparent.**
     b.   Colonel Thomas is a man of **transparent** honesty and loyalty.*
     c.   The homicide* was a **transparent** case of jealousy* that got out of hand.

12.   **scald** (skôld) pour boiling liquid over; burn with hot liquid or steam; heat almost to the boiling point
     a.   Do not neglect* to **scald** the dishes before drying them.
     b.   The **scalding** lava pouring from the mountain placed everyone in peril.*
     c.   By being hasty,* Stella **scalded** her hand.

---

**Which of the words studied in this lesson is suggested by the picture?**

---

*Read the following story to see how the new words are used in it.*

### Roast Beef on Rye

A little digging will **unearth** the roots of our language and habits. For instance, our word "sandwich" is derived from the Earl of Sandwich, who lived in the time of George III. This gentleman would not **depart** from the gambling table for hours on end. If his play happened to **coincide** with dinner, he would **cancel** his regular meal and order a slice of meat to be served to him between two pieces of bread. The biography* of the Earl claims that we are his **debtors** for his discovery of the sandwich. Charles Dickens later used the phrase "sandwich man" to describe someone who walks about with a clearly **legible** message on **placards** hung on his chest and back.

An example of a superstition is the fear of walking under a ladder. This must have been a **contagious** fear for it seems to have started with the ancient belief that spirits lived in trees or wood. "Knocking on wood" was a way of calling up the friendly spirit to protect one from harm. Today a member of the **clergy** might sneer* at this custom, expecting that by this time such superstitions would have receded* into the past with witches and ghosts.

Another expression, "giving someone the cold shoulder," has been traced to the Middle Ages, when a host would serve his guests a cold shoulder of mutton or beef instead of the **customary** hot food. This was a **transparent** attempt to show the guest he was no longer welcome. The host had thus found a more charitable* yet effective way of expressing his feelings without using a **scalding** remark.

**Place one of the new words in each of the blanks below.**

1. After several hours, Raoul abandoned* his search to _____ for home.
2. The police department _____ all leaves until the dangerous lunatic* was captured.
3. The _____ helped to advertise the circus.
4. Since the disease is so _____, it is essential* to identify* the carrier.
5. It was fortunate* that the journalist* had _____ the sinister* plan to assassinate the President.
6. It was _____ for the victorious* general to ride at the head of a parade.
7. When she slipped in the shower, Myra was _____ by the hot water.
8. Through the _____ curtain, the entire scene was visible.*
9. Only a portion of the scrolls found in the cave were _____, but their value should not be underestimated.*
10. The duties of the _____ are not confined* to religious matters.
11. The _____ was brought to court for having deceived* the bank with a false statement of his finances.*
12. Since their interests do not _____, there is still a lingering* doubt in my mind if they should enter into matrimony.*

---

**Matching.** Match the 12 new words in Column I with the definitions in Column II.

| Column I | Column II |
|---|---|
| _____ 1. contagious | a. dig up; discover |
| _____ 2. scald | b. able to be read |
| _____ 3. clergy | c. a notice to be posted |
| _____ 4. cancel | d. usual |
| _____ 5. transparent | e. cross out; call off |
| _____ 6. depart | f. easily spread from one to another |
| _____ 7. unearth | g. pour boiling water over |
| _____ 8. customary | h. easily seen through |
| _____ 9. debtor | i. going away |
| _____ 10. coincide | j. persons prepared for religious work |
| _____ 11. legible | k. person who owes something to another |
| _____ 12. placard | l. correspond exactly |

---

**Spotlight on:**   **legible**—An important idea in vocabulary can be learned with this word. A clear handwriting is described as *legible*—here the word is used *literally*, that is, in its exact, real meaning. When Thomas Wolfe wrote "murder sweltered in his heart and was *legible* upon his face," he used the word *figuratively,* that is, in an imaginative, unusual sense. Many words can be used either literally or figuratively.

# Lesson 40

"He hath heard that men of few words are the best men."

Shakespeare, *Henry V*

1.  **epidemic** (ep ə dem' ik) an outbreak of a disease that spreads rapidly,* so that many people have it at the same time; widespread
    a.  All of the schools in the city were closed during the **epidemic.**
    b.  The depiction* of violence* in the movies has reached **epidemic** proportions.
    c.  During the **epidemic** we were forbidden* to drink water unless it had been boiled.

2.  **obesity** (ō bēs' ə tē) extreme fatness
    a.  **Obesity** is considered* a serious disease.
    b.  The salesman tactfully* referred* to Jack's **obesity** as "stoutness."
    c.  At the medical convention the topic* discussed was the prevention of **obesity.**

3.  **magnify** (mag' nə fī) cause to look larger than it really is; make too much of; go beyond the truth in telling
    a.  A microscope* is a **magnifying** glass.
    b.  It seems that Mr. Steinmetz **magnified** the importance of the document* in his possession.
    c.  Some people have a tendency* to **magnify** every minor* fault in others.

4.  **chiropractor** (kī' rə prak' tər) a person who treats ailments by massage and manipulation of the vertebrae and other forms of therapy on the theory* that disease results from interference with the normal functioning of the nervous system
    a.  The **chiropractor** tried to relieve* the pain by manipulating* the spinal column.
    b.  Mrs. Lehrer confirmed* that a **chiropractor** had been treating her.
    c.  The **chiropractor** recommended hot baths between treatments.

5.  **obstacle** (äb' sti kal) anything that gets in the way or hinders; impediment; obstruction
    a.  The soldiers were compelled* to get over such **obstacles** as ditches and barbed wire.
    b.  Ignorance* is an **obstacle** to progress.
    c.  Prejudice* is often an **obstacle** to harmony* among people.

6.  **ventilate** (ven' tl āt) change the air in; purify by fresh air; discuss openly
    a.  We **ventilated** the kitchen by opening the windows.
    b.  The lungs **ventilate** the blood.
    c.  There is merit* in **ventilating** the topic* of the prom before the entire senior class.

7.  **jeopardize** (jep' ər dīz) risk; endanger
    a.  Soldiers **jeopardize** their lives in war.
    b.  Mr. Marcos revised* his opinion of police officers after two of them had **jeopardized** their lives to save his drowning child.
    c.  Though it **jeopardized** his chance for a promotion,* Mr. Rafael ventured* to criticize his boss.

8.  **negative** (neg' ə tiv) saying no; minus; showing the lights and shadows reversed
    a.  The captain gave a **negative** response* to the request for a leave.
    b.  Three below zero is a **negative** quantity.*
    c.  A **negative** image is used to print a positive picture.

9.  **pension** (pen' shən) regular payment which is not wages; to make such a payment

a. **Pensions** are often paid because of long service, special merit,* or injuries received.

b. The **pension** is calculated* on the basis of your last year's income.

c. Mrs. Colby **pensioned** off her employee after thirty years of loyal* service.

10. **vital** (vī′ tl) having to do with life; necessary to life; causing death, failure or ruin; lively

a. We must preserve* and protect our **vital** resources.

b. Eating is a **vital** function, the obese* man reminded me.

c. The valiant* soldier died of a **vital** wound.

11. **municipal** (mū nis′ əpl) of a city or state; having something to do in the affairs of a city or town

a. The State police assisted the **municipal** police in putting down the riot.

b. There was only a mediocre* turnout for the **municipal** elections.

c. The **municipal** government placed a ban* on parking during business hours.

12. **oral** (ô′ rəl) spoken; using speech; of the mouth

a. An **oral** agreement is not enough; we must have a written promise.

b. **Oral** surgery is necessary to penetrate* to the diseased root.

c. His unique* **oral** powers made Lincoln a man to remember.

---

*Read the following story to see how the new words are used in it.*

**Weight-watchers**

Judging from the popularity* of books on dieting, one would think an **epidemic** of **obesity** is sweeping the nation. Although being fat is not contagious,* it is a condition not to be sneered* at since it affects one-fourth of all Americans. Without **magnifying** the problem, professionals concerned* with the nation's health, from **chiropractors** to medical specialists, agree that being overweight is a major **obstacle** to good health. They point out that people will readily see the need to **ventilate** their homes for fresh air to get rid of vermin* which may cause disease, but they **jeopardize** their health by eating the wrong foods or the wrong amount of foods.

Coincidentally,* a recent survey of employment agencies showed that obesity* has a **negative** effect on a person's chances of landing a job. While the job-seeker is asking about salary and **pensions,** the employer is thinking about the worker's health—and weight is a **vital** consideration when it comes to injuries, disease, and absenteeism.

Some **municipal** jobs, in fact, do require an applicant to be within normal weight range, and one New York bank insists on an **oral** understanding that applicants will take off excess weight. As the *Wall Street Journal* put it, "Fat people often find slim pickings in the job market."

---

**Place one of the new words in each of the blanks below.**

1. Intemperate* eating habits can lead to _____.

2. To avoid* an _____, the Surgeon-General ordered a thorough* study of the situation.

3. At a recent* meeting of _____, a new treatment for arthritis was discussed.

4. The humid* air in this room must be _____.

5. One thousand angry voters loudly signified* an _____ objection to the motion.

6. The frightened man tormented* himself by _____ every unpleasant experience into a calamity.*

7. If used as a precedent,* this verdict* will prove to be an _____ to justice.*

8. Without the_____he had confidently* expected, Mr. Halcroft faced hardships* in his retirement.

9. The sale of the vacant* lot for construction of an office building will _____ the residential character of the neighborhood.

10. Preserve* the _____ in case we need more prints.

11. We should all attend the meeting at the _____ center for the issues are of vital* concern to every citizen.

12. The heart and the brain are considered* the most _____ organs in the human body.

**Which of the words studied in this lesson is suggested by the picture?**

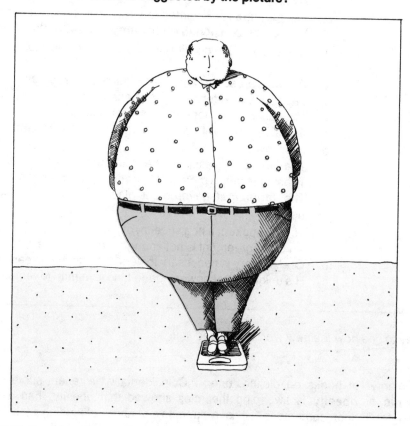

---

### Exercise

*Now make up your own sentences, one for each of the new words you have just been taught.*

1. _____
2. _____
3. _____
4. _____
5. _____
6. _____
7. _____
8. _____
9. _____
10. _____
11. _____
12. _____

---

**Spotlight on:**    **obesity** — Be careful when you refer to your friend's *obesity* that you don't use a word that causes embarrassment. If you call your friend *obese* you'll be using correct medical terminology; however, avoid calling him or her "fat," "chubby," or "corpulent" — words that convey the same idea but in an unpleasant manner.

# Lesson 41

"What care I for words? yet words do well
When he that speaks them pleases those that hear."

Shakespeare, *As You Like It*

**Words To Learn
This Week**

complacent
wasp
rehabilitate
parole
vertical
multitude
nominate
potential
morgue
preoccupied
upholstery
indifference

1. **complacent** (kəm plā′ s'nt) pleased with oneself; self-satisifed
   a. Senator Troy denounced* the **complacent** attitude of the polluters* of our air.
   b. How can you be **complacent** about such a menace?*
   c. I was surprised that Martin was so **complacent** about his brief part in the play.

2. **wasp** (wäsp) an insect with a slender* body and powerful sting
   a. When the **wasps** descended* on the picnic, we ran in all directions.
   b. A swarm* of **wasps** attacked us as we were reclining* on the porch.
   c. The piercing* sting of a **wasp** can be very painful.

3. **rehabilitate** (rē hə bil′ ə tāt) restore to good condition; make over in a new form; restore to former standing, rank, reputation, etc.
   a. The old house was **rehabilitated** at enormous* expense.
   b. The former criminal completely **rehabilitated** himself and was respected by all.
   c. This wing of the house must be **rehabilitated** promptly,* as there is a danger, it will collapse.*

4. **parole** (pə rōl′) word of honor; conditional freedom; to free (a prisoner) under certain conditions
   a. The judge **paroled** the juvenile* offenders on condition that they report to him every three months.
   b. Since the prisoner has been rehabilitated,* his family is exploring* the possibility* of having him **paroled.**
   c. The fugitive* gave his **parole** not to try to escape again.

5. **vertical** (ver′ tə kl) straight up and down with reference to the horizon, for example, a vertical line
   a. It wasn't easy to get the drunken man into a **vertical** position.
   b. The way to vote for your candidate* is to pull the lever from the horizontal position to the **vertical** position.
   c. A circle surrounding a **vertical** line that ends in an inverted V is the well-known peace symbol.*

6. **multitude** (mul′ tə tōō d) a great number; a crowd
   a. A **multitude** of letters kept pouring in to the movie idol.*
   b. The fleeing* culprit* was pursued* by a fierce* **multitude.**
   c. Flood victims were aided by a **multitude** of volunteers.*

7. **nominate** (näm′ ə nāt) name as a candidate for office; appoint to an office
   a. Three times Bryant was **nominated** for office but he was never elected.
   b. The President **nominated** him for Secretary of State.
   c. Though Danny was **nominated** last, he emerged* as the strongest candidate.*

8. **potential** (pə ten′ shəl) possibility* as opposed to actuality; capability of coming into being or action; possible* as opposed to actual; capable of coming into being or action
   a. Mark has the **potential** of being completely rehabilitated.*
   b. The coach felt his team had the **potential** to reach the finals.*
   c. Stockpiling of nuclear weapons represents a **potential** threat* to human survival.*

9. **morgue** (môrg) place where bodies of unknown persons found dead are kept; the reference library of a newspaper office
   a. There is a slender* chance that we can identify* the body in the **morgue.**

127

    b. Bodies in the **morgue** are preserved* by low temperatures.

    c. In the **morgue** of the *New York Times* there are biographies* of most famous people.

10. **preoccupied** (prē äk′ yū pīd) took up all the attention

    a. Getting to school in time for the test **preoccupied** Judy's mind.

    b. My boss is always **preoccupied** with ways of cutting down on the workers' lateness.

    c. Charity* cases **preoccupied** Mrs. Reynaldo's attention.

11. **upholstery** (up hōl′ stər ē) coverings and cushions for furniture

    a. Our old sofa was given new velvet **upholstery.**

    b. The Browns' **upholstery** was so new that we were wary* about visiting them with the children.

    c. Thirty-five dollars was the estimate* for changing the **upholstery** on the dining-room chairs.

12. **indifference** (in dif′ ər əns) lack of interest, care or attention

    a. Allen's **indifference** to his schoolwork worried his parents.

    b. It was a matter of **indifference** to Bernie whether the story circulating* about his engagement was true or not.

    c. My father could not refrain* from commenting on Linda's **indifference** toward her brother's tears.

---

**Which of the words studied in this lesson is suggested by the picture?**

---

*Read the following story to see how the new words are used in it.*

### Where Do We Go from Here?

When we grow too **complacent** with ourselves, along come writers who, **wasp**-like, sting us with reminders of the many problems we face—from **rehabilitating** former prisoners on **parole** to feeding the world's hungry population. Those authors do not see civilization rising almost **vertically** to greater and greater heights. Though **a multitude** of problems beset America, they **nominate** the large urban centers as **potentially** the most dangerous and requiring the most immediate attention. They see the cities as the **morgues** of dead hopes and lost ideals.

We are **preoccupied** with trifles* like the **upholstery** in our homes or personal matters like pension* and benefits, but now we are called upon to contribute to our community on every vital* level—moral.* political, economic. We are not being urged to give up our beloved possessions, but our civilization can be saved only if we overcome the epidemic* of **indifference.** We must begin to live with a new openness to others and a determination to become the best of which we are capable.

## Place one of the new words in each of the blanks below.

1.  The children shrieked* with fear as the _____ flew over them.
2.  It is illegal* to_____a prisoner until he or she has served a minimum* sentence.
3.  The municipal* council voted to _____ the run-down section of the city and to make it a model residential area.
4.  Mike Pavonna was the unanimous* choice of the _____ for the office of mayor.
5.  With all this equipment, we have the _____ to survive* for weeks in the most frigid* climate.
6.  The worn _____ betrayed* the poverty of the family.
7.  His family was distressed at Frank's _____ to the normal adolescent* activities.
8.  Unfortunately,* Carmen was too _____ with dates to devote much time to her studies.
9.  To star the air circulating,* turn the button to a _____ position.
10. Bob was pleased to be _____ for the presidency, but he gallantly* declined in favor of Carole.
11. When the security* leak was discovered, the editor called the newspaper _____ to check if there was any precedent* for such a case.
12. The winner's _____ smile annoyed some of the members of the audience.

---

**Synonyms.** Circle the word that most nearly expresses the meaning of the word printed in heavy black type.

1.  stung by a **wasp**
    a.  remark
    b.  lunatic*
    c.  tragedy*
    d.  traitor*
    e.  insect

2.  voters who are too **complacent** to change
    a.  self-satisfied
    b.  assertive
    c.  bewildered*
    d.  distressed*
    e.  juvenile*

3.  the candidate **nominated** for office
    a.  encouraged*
    b.  underestimated*
    c.  designated
    d.  employed
    e.  motivated

4.  furniture **upholstery**
    a.  material
    b.  antiques
    c.  wax
    d.  style
    e.  comfort

5.  **rehabilitate** a drug-user
    a.  punish*
    b.  unearth*
    c.  locate*
    d.  restore
    e.  upset

6.  **vertical** lines
    a.  curved
    b.  jagged*
    c.  hidden
    d.  lengthwise
    e.  sideways

7.  **preoccupied** with thoughts of the work ahead of him
    a.  absorbed
    b.  affected
    c.  amused
    d.  covered
    e.  lost

8.  a **multitude** of sins
    a.  great number
    b.  thorough* review
    c.  total destruction
    d.  valid* criticism
    e.  strong conviction

9.  **potential** earnings
    a.  easily financed*
    b.  economical* and inst
    c.  possible as opposed
    d.  miserly*
    e.  repeatedly jeopardi

10. bodies kept in the **mor** for identification
    a.  undertaker's esta
    b.  camp grounds
    c.  office building
    d.  rooming house
    e.  health resort

11. **indifference** to p
    a.  inattention
    b.  sympathy
    c.  vulnerability
    d.  tendency*
    e.  prejudice

12. out on **parole**
    a.  appeal*
    b.  conditio
    c.  conflicti
    d.  confine
    e.  reduce

---

**Spotlight on:**   **wasp**—Newspaper writers enjoy taking the first letters of titles or express
word from them. While a *wasp* is certainly an insect, it also, when spelled
Women's Air Service Pilots or White-Anglo-Saxon-Protestant. Since a was
people with affection, you can imagine that the acronym (a word made u
was not meant as a compliment to female pilots or Protestants.

# Lesson 42

1. **maintain** (mān tān′) keep; keep up; carry on; uphold; support; declare to be true
   a. Angelo **maintained** his hold on the jagged* rock though his fingers were becoming numb.*
   b. The judge **maintained** his opinion that the verdict* was fair.
   c. The pauper* was unable to **maintain** his family without the help of charity.*

2. **snub** (snub) treat coldly, scornfully or with contempt; cold treatment
   a. Darryl later apologized* to Sally for **snubbing** her at the dance.
   b. Sandra was tormented* by the thought that she might be **snubbed** by her classmates.
   c. I considered* it a rude **snub** when I was not invited to the party.

3. **endure** (en dyùr′ or en door′) last; keep on; undergo; bear; stand
   a. How can you **endure** such disrespect?
   b. The valiant* officer **endured** much pain.
   c. Dr. Hardy was confident* he could **endure** the hardships* of space travel.

4. **wrath** (rath) very great anger; rage
   a. Anticipating* Father's **wrath,** we tried to give him the news slowly.
   b. There is no rage* like the **wrath** of an angry bear.
   c. After Ernie's **wrath** subsided,* we were able to tell him what happened.

5. **expose** (eks pōz′) lay open; uncover; leave unprotected; show openly
   a. Soldiers in an open field are **exposed** to the enemy's gunfire.
   b. Foolish actions **expose** a person to the sneers* of others.
   c. The article **exposed** the vital* document* as a forgery.

6. **legend** (lej′ ənd) story coming from the past, which many people have believed; what is written on a coin or below a picture
   a. Stories about King Arthur and his knights are popular* **legends.**
   b. **Legend** has exaggerated* the size of Paul Bunyan.
   c. The **legend** on the rare coin was scarcely* legible.*

7. **ponder** (pän′ dər) consider carefully
   a. Not wishing to act hastily,* the governor **pondered** the problem for days.
   b. After **pondering** the question, the board decided to grant the parole.*
   c. The villagers, faced with a famine,* **pondered** their next move.

**resign** (ri zīn′) give up; yield; submit
   Vito **resigned** his position as editor* of the school paper.
   Upon hearing the news of the defeat, the football coach promptly* **resigned.**
   Ipon examining the injury, the chiropractor* told Jim he had better **resign**
   nself to a week in bed.

(dras′ tik) acting with force or violence*
   olice took **drastic** measures to end the crime wave.
   ost **drastic** changes in centuries* have taken place during our life

rests of justice,* **drastic** action must be taken.
platform built on the shore or out from the shore beside which
unload
he exhausted* laborers unloading the cargo on the **wharf.**
isted* that his client* was never seen near the **wharf** where
ken place.
ne **wharf** for the supply ships to unload was a starving
ue* of people.

11. **amend** (ə mend') change for the better; correct; change
    a. It is time you **amended** your ways.
    b. Each time they **amended** the plan, they made it worse.
    c. Rather than **amend** the club's constitution again, let us discard* it and start afresh.

12. **ballot** (bal' ət) piece of paper used in voting; the whole number of votes cast; the method of secret voting; to vote or decide by using ballots
    a. Clyde, confident* of victory, dropped his **ballot** into the box.
    b. After we counted the **ballots** a second time, Leo's victory was confirmed.*
    c. To avoid embarrassing the candidates,* we **ballot** instead of showing hands.

---

*Read the following story to see how the new words are used in it.*

### A Time for Decision

Carl Brown walked wearily* from the bus stop, his thoughts preoccupied* with the day's events. He had become accustomed to receiving the blame for his colleagues'* mistakes. He could remain complacent* when less deserving workers were promoted* ahead of him. He could even **maintain** an air of indifference* when the young man he had trained now **snubbed** him. What he could not **endure** was the ridicule of his fellow employees.* His **wrath** flamed at the thought that his secret had been **exposed**. The **legend** of his honesty had died.

Carl Brown **pondered** his next move. Should he **resign** or take even more **drastic** measures? His steps led past the **wharf** where the ships were unloading their cargoes of fruit. He looked into the dark waters and took a deep breath. No, this was not a sin that could be erased. He heaved a sigh and determined to **amend** his ways. Never again would he sign his **ballot** "Carl Smith."

---

**Which of the words studied in this lesson is suggested by the picture?**

**Place one of the new words in each of the blanks below.**

1. When the third person she approached turned away from her, Marilyn had a vague* feeling she was being _____.

2. Achilles' _____ did not cease* until he had taken revenge on the slayer of his friend.

3. As the captain _____ their situation, he realized that resistance* was in vain.*

4. Father _____ that all forms of gambling should be declared illegal.*

5. The prophet warned that the land cannot _____ such violations of morality.*

6. To diminish* the chances of raising weaklings, the ancient Spartans used to _____ to the elements the babies that they did not want.

7. The Robin Hood stories are a good illustration* of a _____ from the Middle Ages.

8. The _____ is the symbol* of the democratic way of choosing leaders.

9. Because of the secret nature of the cargo, visits to the _____ area were prohibited.*

10. The patriot* was _____ dying for his deed.

11. We are trying to persuade* the sponsors of the bill to _____ it in order to improve its chances for passage.

12. The guinea pigs could not put up with _____ changes in their diet.

---

**Exercise**

*Now make up your own sentences, one for each of the new words you have just been taught.*

1. _____
2. _____
3. _____
4. _____
5. _____
6. _____
7. _____
8. _____
9. _____
10. _____
11. _____
12. _____

---

**Spotlight on:**    **ballot** — This method of voting derives its name from the small balls (or stones) that were placed secretly in a box, a practice that is still used in some organizations even today. In city, state, and national elections, voting machines seem to be used in densely populated areas, but in farm towns and small cities, voters still drop their *ballots* (paper) in a box.

# Word Review #7

These exercises are based on some of the words which you found in Lessons 37–42.

**A.** In each of the parentheses below there are two choices. Pick the one that fits better.
1. It was (legible, customary) for Mrs. Thorpe to leave her baby at our house when she went shopping.
2. Only a (drastic, deliberate) change in the weather can save our city from the flood.
3. Don't (jeopardize, rehabilitate) your future by doing something now that you may be sorry for later.
4. After the (parole, tumult) died down, the prisoners went back to their cells quietly.
5. Lucille thought that she could (ponder, endure) great pain, but a visit to the dentist changed her mind.
6. While walking across the lawn, I got (drenched, scalded) by the cold water sprinkler.
7. After the waters (receded, abided), we walked up and down the beach looking for interesting shells.
8. Our chances for success (dwindled, coincided) with each passing day.
9. When Sheldon reached the (summit, potential) of the mountain, he rested before trying to come down.
10. I was too (resigned, preoccupied) with my work to pay attention to the television set.

**B. Opposites.** In Column I are ten words from Lessons 37–42. Match them correctly with their *opposite* meanings in Column II.

| Column I | Column II |
|---|---|
| 1. surplus | a. shortage |
| 2. heed | b. bury |
| 3. unearth | c. written |
| 4. magnify | d. refuse to listen |
| 5. amend | e. leave the same |
| 6. oral | f. arrive |
| 7. depart | g. split-up |
| 8. unify | h. happiness |
| 9. wrath | i. stand up straight |
| 10. kneel | j. make smaller |

**C.** Which of the vocabulary choices in parentheses fits best in these newspaper headlines?
1. **Search Is On For _____ To Millionaire's Fortune**     (Verdict, Heir, Obstacle, Surplus)
2. **False "Arabs" _____ Member Of Congress**     (Heed, Expose, Endure, Ponder)
3. **_____ Of Measles Breaks Out In County**     (Summit, Swarm, Potential, Epidemic)
4. **Accused Of _____ Attempt To Sell Secrets**     (Legible, Customary, Majestic, Deliberate)
5. **_____ History Of Tribe To Be Tape-Recorded**     (Oral, Drastic, Complacent, Negative)
6. **Bad Economic News Causes _____ At Stock Market**     (Charity, Multitude, Verdict, Tumult)
7. **Mayor Refuses To _____ By Previous Agreement**     (Unify, Abide, Recede, Snub)
8. **Forced To _____ Tonight's Show, Apologizes Producer**     (Magnify, Cancel, Unify, Nominate)
9. **Prisons Fail To _____, Charges Social Work Expert**     (Rehabilitate, Jeopardize, Amend, Dwindle)
10. **_____ Tells Life Story of Reggie Jackson**     (Clergy, Ballot, Biography, Indifference)

**D.** From the list of words below choose the word that means:
1. the exercise of a democratic privilege *and* may be done by sophisticated machinery or simply by a piece of paper
2. a stinging insect *and also* is a well-known acronym, an abbreviation whose letters stand for the name of a group
3. a condition caused by overeating *and* comes from a Latin word meaning "To eat away"
4. can be read *but* figuratively can mean able to be clearly seen or noticed
5. a person who defaces or damages public property *and* is based on the name of a German tribe that destroyed Rome in A.D. 455
6. gradually decrease to a vanishing point *and* rhymes with *swindle*
7. move like a dazed boxer *and also* may refer to the trembling or shaking of one's voice
8. saturate or wet through and through *and* is closely related to the word *drink*
9. a story handed down from early times *as well as* a key or explanation on a map, or picture
10. restore a person to usefulness and normalcy *as well as* restore a building or a neighborhood that has fallen upon bad times

| | | | | | |
|---|---|---|---|---|---|
| vandal | wobble | indifference | endure | placard | rehabilitate |
| legend | coincide | swarm | tumult | resign | municipal |
| complacent | drench | maintain | transparent | verdict | wasp |
| abide | nominate | snub | legible | pension | contagious |
| multitude | potential | dwindle | obesity | ballot | surplus |

# Answers

**Lesson 1:** 1. data 2. tact 3. vacant 4. oath 5. jealous 6. gallant 7. hardship 8. abandon 9. qualify 10. keen 11. Unaccustomed 12. bachelor
1. oath 2. keen 3. abandon 4. hardship 5. qualify 6. jealous 7. gallant 8. bachelor 9. data 10. tact 11. vacant 12. unaccustomed
The illustration suggests the word **vacant.**

**Lesson 2:** 1. dismal 2. wager 3. peril 4. recline 5. shriek 6. sinister 7. conceal 8. inhabit 9. frigid 10. numb 11. corpse 12. tempt
The illustration suggests the word **wager.**

**Lesson 3:** 1. annual 2. blend 3. minimum 4. beau 5. persuade 6. visible 7. typical 8. devise 9. essential 10. wholesale 11. scarce 12. expensive
The illustration suggests the word **expensive.**

**Lesson 4:** 1. humid 2. vanish 3. dense 4. predict 5. villain 6. Vapor 7. enormous 8. theory 9. utilize 10. descend 11. eliminate 12. circulate
1. b 2. b 3. d 4. b 5. c 6. a 7. b 8. c 9. c 10. c 11. c 12. b
The illustration suggests the word **predict.**

**Lesson 5:** 1. rural 2. campus 3. evade 4. majority 5. assemble 6. tradition 7. burden 8. explore 9. reform 10. topic 11. probe 12. debate
The illustration suggests the word **debate.**

**Lesson 6:** 1. thorough *or* comprehensive 2. undoubtedly 3. approach 4. popular 5. neglect 6. employee 7. defect 8. deceive *or* defraud 9. deceived 10. detect 11. client 12. comprehensive or thorough
1. popular 2. employees 3. detected 4. approached 5. comprehensive 6. defect 7. undoubtedly 8. thorough 9. neglect 10. defraud 11. deceive 12. clients
The illustration suggests the word **employee.**

**Word Review #1:** A. 1. typical 2. blend 3. peril 4. detected 5. neglect 6. sinister 7. qualify 8. unaccustomed 9. scarce 10. reform
B. 1. g 2. j 3. a 4. c 5. b 6. d 7. i 8. e 9. f 10. h
C. 1. abandon 2. minimum 3. dense 4. neglect 5. evade 6. campus 7. oath 8. descend 9. vacant 10. predict
D. 1. wholesale 2. villain 3. majority 4. probe 5. defraud 6. abandon 7. assemble 8. eliminate 9. comprehensive 10. tact

**Lesson 7:** 1. preserve 2. gloomy 3. consent 4. unique 5. resent 6. denounced 7. molested 8. unforeseen 9. torrent 10. postponed 11. capsule 12. massive
The illustration suggests the word **postponed.**

**Lesson 8:** 1. weird 2. valid 3. obvious 4. mediocre 5. reluctant 6. exaggerate 7. security 8. bulky 9. amateur 10. variety 11. prominent 12. survive
1. f 2. d 3. h 4. g 5. j 6. a 7. l 8. b 9. k 10. i 11. e 12. c
The illustration suggests the word **exaggerate.**

**Lesson 9:** 1. ignore 2. documents 3. century 4. challenge 5. source 6. conclude 7. undeniable 8. lack 9. vicinity 10. rage 11. miniature 12. resist
1. c 2. a 3. d 4. a 5. c 6. c 7. b 8. a 9. d 10. a 11. c 12. a
The illustration suggests the word **rage.**

**Lesson 10:** 1. menace 2. dread 3. tendency 4. underestimate 5. excel 6. flabby 7. numerous 8. feminine 9. compete 10. mount 11. victorious 12. masculine
The illustration suggests the word **victorious.**

**Lesson 11:** 1. decades 2. vision 3. minority 4. glimpse 5. absurd 6. frequent 7. hesitate 8. solitary 9. conflict 10. Recent 11. evidence 12. fiction
1. h 2. g 3. b 4. k 5. i 6. d 7. j 8. a 9. f 10. e 11. c 12. l
The illustration suggests the word **vision.**

**Lesson 12:** 1. frank 2. audible 3. urgent 4. urban 5. ignite 6. prohibited 7. pollute 8. decrease 9. abolish 10. population 11. reveals 12. adequate
1. urban 2. reveal 3. adequate 4. pollute 5. abolish 6. decrease 7. frank 8. urgent 9. ignite 10. population 11. audible 12. prohibit
The illustration suggests the word **pollute**

**Word Review #2:** A. 1. postpone 2. underestimated 3. mediocre 4. menace 5. challenged 6. prominent 7. abolished 8. Unforeseen 9. adequate 10. ignores
B. 1. d 2. j 3. a 4. h 5. b 6. i 7. c 8. g 9. e 10. f
C. 1. absurd 2. prohibit 3. postpone 4. reveal 5. decade 6. prominent 7. menace 8. massive 9. urban 10. gloomy
D. 1. hesitate 2. fiction 3. massive 4. century 5. conclude 6. absurd 7. obvious 8. preserve 9. vision 10. unique

**Lesson 13:** 1. commence 2. migrate 3. gleam 4. famine 5. vessel 6. identify 7. observant 8. editor 9. revive 10. persist 11. Hazy 12. journalist
The illustration suggests the word **journalist.**

**Lesson 14:** 1. unruly 2. brutal, violent, *or* vicious 3. brawl 4. thrust 5. duplicate 6. rival *or* opponent 7. rival *or* opponent 8. bewildered 9. underdog 10. brutal, violent, *or* vicious 11. whirling 12. brutal, violent *or* vicious
1. T 2. F 3. T 4. T 5. T 6. F 7. F 8. T 9. F 10. F 11. T 12. T
The illustration suggests the word **bewildered.**

**Lesson 15:** 1. fortunate 2. sacred 3. revise *or* alter 4. innovative 5. pursue 6. mature 7. unanimous 8. pledge 9. revise *or* alter 10. pioneers 11. casual 12. expand
The illustration suggests the word **pledge.**

**Lesson 16:** 1. grateful 2. doubt 3. slender 4. cautious 5. accurate 6. penetrate *or* pierce 7. vast 8. surpass 9. capacity 10. confident 11. microscope 12. pierce
1. a 2. c 3. a 4. d 5. a 6. b 7. a 8. a 9. c 10. b 11. a 12. a
The illustration suggests the word pierce or **penetrate.**

**Lesson 17:** 1. avoid 2. aware 3. quantity 4. appeal 5. wretched 6. harsh 7. misfortune 8. opt 9. wary 10. keg 11. nourish 12. addict
1. j 2. i 3. k 4. l 5. a 6. h 7. c 8. e 9. b 10. f 11. g 12. d
The illustration suggests the word **keg.**

---

**Lesson 18:** 1. reckless 2. ingenious 3. economical 4. rave 5. glance 6. budget 7. manipulate 8. lubricate 9. tragedy 10. horrid 11. pedestrian 12. nimble
The illustration suggests the word **lubricate.**

---

**Word Review #3:** A. 1. famine 2. nimble 3. revive 4. mature 5. alter 6. reckless 7. pursue 8. economical 9. unanimously 10. capacity
B. 1. c 2. a 3. j 4. f 5. d 6. b 7. e 8. i 9. h 10. g
C. 1. famine 2. unanimous 3. pioneer 4. migrate 5. revive 6. wary 7. unruly 8. slender 9. reckless 10. vicious
D. 1. confidence 2. pioneer 3. rival 4. vessel 5. thrust 6. revise 7. capacity 8. nourish 9. tragedy 10. rave

**Lesson 19:** 1. ban 2. quota 3. abundant 4. absorbed 5. appropriate 6. estimate 7. uneasy 8. panic 9. harvest 10. calculated 11. morsel 12. threat
1. abundant 2. threat 3. uneasy 4. panic 5. harvest 6. calculate 7. ban 8. morsel 9. absorb 10. quotas 11. estimate 12. appropriate
The illustration suggests the word **panic.**

**Lesson 20:** 1. perish 2. jagged 3. captive 4. crafty 5. linger 6. defiant 7. ambush 8. prosper 9. emerged 10. devour 11. vigor 12. fragile
1. a 2. b 3. a 4. b 5. d 6. b 7. b 8. d 9. a 10. a 11. a 12. b
The illustration suggests the word **captive.**

**Lesson 21:** 1. transmitted 2. confirm *or* verify 3. detour 4. weary 5. merit 6. plea 7. collide 8. relieved 9. dilemma 10. confirm *or* verify 11. baffled 12. anticipate
1. detour 2. plea 3. collide 4. transmit 5. baffle 6. merit 7. relieve 8. weary 9. confirm 10. dilemma 11. verify 12. anticipate
The illustration suggests the word **collide.**

**Lesson 22:** 1. delinquent 2. penalize 3. vocation 4. homicide 5. acknowledge 6. reject 7. warden 8. spouse 9. unstable 10. deprived 11. Justice 12. beneficiary
1. c 2. h 3. k 4. f 5. j 6. i 7. a 8. b 9. d 10. g 11. l 12. e
The illustration suggests the word **reject.**

**Lesson 23:** 1. embraced 2. forbid 3. proceed 4. reptile 5. partial 6. logical 7. rarely 8. exhibit 9. prior 10. precaution 11. valiant 12. extract
The illustration suggests the word **extract.**

**Lesson 24:** 1. authority 2. encourage 3. symbol 4. vermin 5. neutral 6. consider 7. fierce 8. wail 9. trifle 10. detest 11. scowl 12. sneer
1. c 2. a 3. c 4. a 5. c 6. b 7. d 8. a 9. c 10. a 11. a 12. b
The illustration suggests the word **wail.**

**Word Review #4:** A. 1. quotas 2. reject 3. fragile 4. extract 5. dilemma 6. partial 7. linger 8. neutral 9. calculated 10. confirmed
B. 1. f 2. h 3. d 4. b 5. j 6. c 7. i 8. e 9. a 10. g
C. 1. exhibit 2. fragile 3. collide 4. dilemma 5. vermin 6. confirm 7. prosper 8. perish 9. quota 10. abundant
D. 1. ambush 2. beneficiary 3. symbol 4. harvest 5. panic 6. prosper 7. battle 8. warden 9. precaution 10. trifle

**Lesson 25:** 1. baggage 2. calamity 3. paupers 4. collapse 5. architect 6. prosecuted 7. squander 8. fugitive 9. bigamy 10. abroad 11. envy 12. matrimony
The illustration suggests the word **baggage.**

**Lesson 26:** 1. quench 2. guide 3. respond 4. beckoned 5. venture 6. compelled 7. awesome 8. betrayed 9. possible 10. pacify 11. uttered 12. awkward
1. F 2. T 3. F 4. T 5. T 6. F 7. T 8. T 9. F 10. T 11. F 12. T
The illustration suggests the word **quench.**

**Lesson 27:** 1. feeble 2. ceased 3. rash 4. exhausted 5. monarch 6. disrupt 7. thrifty 8. rapidly 9. severity 10. unite 11. Despite 12. miserly
The illustration suggests the word **monarch.**

**Lesson 28:** 1. undernourished 2. disclose 3. disaster 4. outlaw 5. excessive 6. culprit 7. promote 8. illustrate 9. insist 10. censor 11. juvenile 12. bait
1. bait 2. promote 3. culprit 4. insist 5. outlaw 6. juvenile 7. censor 8. disclose 9. excessive 10. disaster 11. illustrate 12. undernourished
The illustration suggests the word **disaster.**

**Lesson 29:** 1. exempt 2. repetition 3. blundered
4. comprehend 5. toiled 6. maimed 7. commended
8. final 9. mourning 10. vain 11. subsided 12. daze
1. i 2. f 3. h 4. l 5. g 6. j 7. b 8. d 9. e 10. a
11. k 12. c
The illustration suggests the word **mourning.**

**Lesson 30:** 1. appointed 2. mortal 3. occupants
4. depict 5. site 6. verse 7. quartered 8. quoted
9. novel 10. attracted 11. morality 12. roam
The illustration suggests the word **novel.**

**Word Review #5**· A. 1. prosecuted 2. depict
3. blunder 4. mourn 5. squandered 6. utter 7. guide
8. matrimony 9. novel 10. unite
B. 1. f 2. a 3. i 4. j 5. h 6. d 7. b 8. c 9. e 10. g
C. 1. subside 2. juvenile 3. pacify 4. mourn 5. cease
6. monarch 7. unite 8. depict 9. thrifty 10. bigamy
D. 1. mortal 2. maim 3. calamity 4. thrifty 5. architect
6. bigamist 7. quench 8. monarch 9. censor 10. quarter

**Lesson 31:** 1. idle 2. dispute 3. commuter 4. valor
5. vein 6. uneventful 7. lunatic 8. jest 9. confine
10. patriotic 11. fertile 12. idol
The illustration suggests the word **commuter.**

**Lesson 32:** 1. distress 2. maximum 3. flee
4. tormenting 5. loyalty 6. apologize 7. colleagues
8. signified 9. refer 10. diminished 11. mythology
12. vulnerable
1. signify 2. flee 3. distress 4. maximum 5. refer
6. loyalty 7. colleague 8. mythology 9. vulnerable
10. torment 11. diminish 12. apologize
The illustration suggests the word **flee.**

**Lesson 33:** 1. mumbled 2. wad 3. retain 4. volunteers
5. jolly 6. prejudice 7. hindered 8. mute
9. abused 10. shrill 11. lecture 12. witty
The illustration suggests the word **lecture.**

**Lesson 34:** 1. adolescent 2. candidate 3. radical
4. spontaneous 5. vaccinated 6. utensil 7. sensitive
8. temperate 9. untidy 10. coeducational 11. precedes
12. skim
1. k 2. e 3. d 4. b 5. j 6. i 7. c 8. g 9. l 10. h 11. a
12. f
The illustration suggests the word **vaccinate.**

**Lesson 35:** 1. lottery 2. obtain 3. cinema 4. event
5. soaring 6. stationary 7. Subsequent 8. discard
9. relate 10. vague 11. finance 12. elevate
1. elevate 2. subsequent 3. cinema 4. event 5. soar 6. vague
7. stationary 8. lottery 9. relate 10. obtain 11. finance
12. discard
The illustration suggests the word **lottery.**

**Lesson 36:** 1. prompt 2. soothed 3. redeemed 4. refrain
5. harmony 6. hasty 7. tempered 8. scorch 9. sympathetic
10. resumed 11. illegal 12. narcotics
The illustration suggests the word **scorch.**

**Word Review #6:** A. 1. relate 2. prompt 3. vague
4. obtain 5. resume 6. distressed 7. vulnerable
8. radical 9. uneventful 10. maximum
B. 1. g 2. j 3. a 4. i 5. e 6. b 7. h 8. c 9. f 10. d
C. 1. vaccinate 2. idle 3. diminished 4. resume 5. prejudice
6. radical 7. idol 8. vulnerable 9. uneventful 10. commuter
D. 1. lunatic 2. colleague 3. prejudice 4. vaccinate 5. cinema
6. mute 7. spontaneous 8. lottery 9. discard 10. redeem

**Lesson 37:** 1. dwindled 2. heir 3. deliberate 4. surplus
5. heeding 6. unified 7. vandals 8. abide 9. drought
10. summit 11. traitor 12. majestic
1. a 2. b 3. d 4. a 5. e 6. b 7. a 8. a 9. d 10. b
11. e 12. e
The illustration suggests the word **summit.**

**Lesson 38:** 1. tumult 2. swarm 3. verdict 4. biography
5. receded 6. charity 7. kneel 8. dejected 9. tyrant
10. drenched 11. wobbled 12. obedient
1. F 2. T 3. F 4. T 5. T 6. F 7. T 8. T 9 F. 10. F
11. T 12. T
The illustration suggests the word **kneel.**

**Lesson 39:** 1. depart 2. cancelled 3. placard 4. contagious
5. unearthed 6. customary 7. scalded 8. transparent
9. legible 10. clergy 11. debtor 12. coincide
1. f 2. g 3. j 4. e 5. h 6. i 7. a 8. d 9. k 10 l 11. b
12. c
The illustration suggests the word **depart.**

**Lesson 40:** 1. obesity 2. epidemic 3. chiropractors
4. ventilated 5. oral 6. magnifying 7. obstacle
8. pension 9. jeopardize 10. negative 11. municipal
12. vital
The illustration suggests the word **obesity.**

**Lesson 41:**· 1. wasp 2. parole 3. rehabilitate 4. multitude 5. potential 6. upholstery 7. indifference
8. preoccupied 9. vertical 10. nominated 11. morgue
12. complacent
1. e 2. a 3. c 4. a 5. d 6. d 7. a 8. a 9. c 10. a
11. a 12. b
The illustration suggests the word **parole.**

**Lesson 42:** 1. snubbed 2. wrath 3. pondered 4. maintained
5. endure 6. expose 7. legend 8. ballot 9. wharf 10. resigned
11. amend 12. drastic
The illustration suggests the word **ballot.**

**Word Review #7:** A. 1. customary 2. drastic 3. jeopardize 4. tumult 5. endure 6. drenched 7. receded
8. dwindled 9. summit 10. preoccupied
B. 1. a 2. d 3. b 4. j 5. e 6. c 7. f 8. g 9. h 10. i
C. 1. heir 2. expose 3. epidemic 4. deliberate 5. oral
6. tumult 7. abide 8. cancel 9. rehabilitate 10. biography
D. 1. ballot 2. wasp 3. obesity 4. legible 5. vandal 6. dwindle
7. wobble 8. drench 9. legend 10. rehabilitate

# Index

The number indicates the lesson in which the word first appears.

# Introducing
# Barron's Book Notes
## The Smart Way to Study Literature

Everything you need for better understanding, better performance in class, better grades! Clear concise, fun to read—Barron's Book Notes make literature come alive.

**101 titles to choose from:**

THE AENEID
ALL QUIET ON THE WESTERN FRONT
ALL THE KING'S MEN
ANIMAL FARM
ANNA KARENINA
AS I LAY DYING
AS YOU LIKE IT
BABBITT
BEOWULF
BILLY BUDD & TYPEE
BRAVE NEW WORLD
CANDIDE
CANTERBURY TALES
CATCH-22
THE CATCHER IN THE RYE
CRIME AND PUNISHMENT
THE CRUCIBLE
CRY, THE BELOVED COUNTRY
DAISY MILLER &
   TURN OF THE SCREW
DAVID COPPERFIELD
DEATH OF A SALESMAN
THE DIVINE COMEDY: THE INFERNO
DOCTOR FAUSTUS
A DOLL'S HOUSE & HEDDA GABLER
DON QUIXOTE
ETHAN FROME
A FAREWELL TO ARMS
FAUST: PARTS I AND II
FOR WHOM THE BELL TOLLS
THE GLASS MENAGERIE &
   A STREETCAR NAMED DESIRE
THE GOOD EARTH
THE GRAPES OF WRATH
GREAT EXPECTATIONS
THE GREAT GATSBY
GULLIVER'S TRAVELS

HAMLET
HARD TIMES
HEART OF DARKNESS &
   THE SECRET SHARER
HENRY IV, PART I
THE HOUSE OF THE SEVEN GABLES
HUCKLEBERRY FINN
THE ILIAD
INVISIBLE MAN
JANE EYRE
JULIUS CAESAR
THE JUNGLE
KING LEAR
LIGHT IN AUGUST
LORD JIM
LORD OF THE FLIES
THE LORD OF THE RINGS &
   THE HOBBIT
MACBETH
MADAME BOVARY
THE MAYOR OF CASTERBRIDGE
THE MERCHANT OF VENICE
A MIDSUMMER NIGHT'S DREAM
MOBY DICK
MY ANTONIA
NATIVE SON & BLACK BOY
NEW TESTAMENT
1984
THE ODYSSEY
OEDIPUS TRILOGY
OF MICE AND MEN
THE OLD MAN AND THE SEA
OLD TESTAMENT
OLIVER TWIST
ONE FLEW OVER THE
   CUCKOO'S NEST
OTHELLO

OUR TOWN
PARADISE LOST
THE PEARL
PORTRAIT OF THE ARTIST
   AS A YOUNG MAN
PRIDE AND PREJUDICE
THE PRINCE
THE RED BADGE OF COURAGE
THE REPUBLIC
RETURN OF THE NATIVE
RICHARD III
ROMEO AND JULIET
THE SCARLET LETTER
A SEPARATE PEACE
SILAS MARNER
SLAUGHTERHOUSE FIVE
SONS AND LOVERS
THE SOUND AND THE FURY
STEPPENWOLF & SIDDHARTHA
THE STRANGER
THE SUN ALSO RISES
A TALE OF TWO CITIES
THE TAMING OF THE SHREW
THE TEMPEST
TESS OF THE D'URBERVILLES
TO KILL A MOCKINGBIRD
TOM JONES
TOM SAWYER
TWELFTH NIGHT
UNCLE TOM'S CABIN
WALDEN
WHO'S AFRAID OF
   VIRGINIA WOOLF?
WUTHERING HEIGHTS

**Only $2.50 each!**
**Canada $3.50**
**On sale at your local bookstore**

All prices subject to change without notice. At your bookstore, or order direct from Barron's. Add 10% for postage and handling (minimum charge $1.50, Can. $2.00), N.Y. residents add sales tax.

**BARRON'S**

Barron's Educational Series, Inc.
P.O. Box 8040, 250 Wireless Blvd., Hauppauge, NY 11788
In Canada: Georgetown Book Warehouse
34 Armstrong Ave., Georgetown, Ont. L7G 4R9

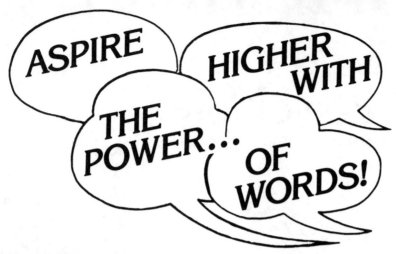

ASPIRE HIGHER WITH THE POWER... OF WORDS!

### 504 ABSOLUTELY ESSENTIAL WORDS
*$6.95, Can. $9.95 (3702-2)*
Builds practical vocabulary skills through funny stories and cartoons plus practice exercises.

### BUILDING AN EFFECTIVE VOCABULARY
*$8.95, Can. $11.95 (2041-3)*
Covers all the methods of evaluating words to improve communication skills.

### 1001 PITFALLS IN ENGLISH GRAMMAR
*$8.95, Can. $11.95 (3719-7)*
Examines the most common errors in the English language.

### 1100 WORDS YOU NEED TO KNOW
*$6.95, Can. $9.95 (2264-5)*
This book is the way to master more than 1100 useful words and idioms taken from the mass media.

### WORD MASTERY: A Guide to the
**Understanding of Words** *$6.95, Can. $9.95 (0526-0)*
Enhances word use and word development through the presentation of words in such natural settings as newspapers and magazines. Practice exercises are included.

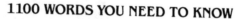

### WRITE YOUR WAY INTO COLLEGE
*$7.95, Can. $10.95 (2997-6)*
A step-by-step guide to writing an effective college application essay. Actual student essays are included with helpful critiques.

### GETTING YOUR WORDS ACROSS
*$7.95, Can. $10.95 (2082-0)*
The unique basic vocabulary book that uses brief articles, exercises and crossword puzzles to build word power.

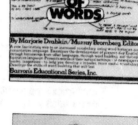

### HANDBOOK OF COMMONLY USED
**AMERICAN IDIOMS** *$5.95, Can. $7.95 (2816-3)*
With 1500 popular idioms, this book will benefit both English-speaking people and those learning English as a second language.

**BARRON'S EDUCATIONAL SERIES**
250 Wireless Boulevard
Hauppauge, New York 11788
Canada: Georgetown Book Warehouse
34 Armstrong Avenue
Georgetown, Ontario L7G 4R9

Prices subject to change without notice. Books may be purchased at your bookstore, or by mail from Barron's. Enclose check or money order for total amount plus sales tax where applicable and 10% for postage and handling (minimum charge $1.50, Can. $2.00). All books are paperback editions.